SAVED

BY

GRACE

THE PARADOX OF MALE

CHILD SYNDROME

*A real-life story of the ordeals, hardships
and challenges of females living in
a community that has male preferences.*

MRS LOIS HEMBADOON ADURA ESQ.

**FLOREAT SYSTEMS
PUBLICATIONS**
BENIN CITY

© 2020
Lois Hembadoon Adura Esq.

ISBN:
979-867-172-808-8

*****

Printed by:
Floreat Systems,
Catholic Archdiocese of Benin Printing Press
30, Airport Road, Benin City,
Edo State, Nigeria

Distributed Nationwide by:
Epret Hills Consult Limited
Pickups, Deliveries, Grocery Shopping etc.
No 2, Road 2, Bmuko, Opposite Graceland School,
Zone A, Dutse, FCT - Abuja
+234 803 915 5427, +234 703 116 1161

FOREWORD

"When you are destined to be fruitful, it doesn't matter whether the world cuts your branches. No one can stop the will of God. My mother is a living testimony".

You have heard of Superman, Batman, and Wonder Woman. You must have also heard or read about how they save the world and keep everyone safe. But my mother is the biggest superhero I've ever met. She cares about everyone and won't let you struggle if she can help it. She's a better superhero than any Marvel or DC character because she loves people. Not all heroes wear capes! Here is one such.

Her love makes such a big impact on everyone so that you are not left the same after meeting her. The day you meet my mother is the day you can never forget. She radiates such a silently roaring happiness and whenever she talks, a song of joy and patience replaces it. She cares for people with a natural passion - from looking after her sisters to making my brother pancakes to making sure I've eaten my breakfast. It's just something you can't ignore about her. I am so grateful to God for giving me such a beautiful mother.

I will be honest with you, I don't know half of the struggles my mother has been through, but I know it has turned her into a God-fearing, strong, and tough-skinned woman. The only other thing I know is that getting through all of that, and still being able to smile about it, is testament to the work of God in her life. How do you explain how one person can show so much love to others? How do you explain her sacrificing everything for her friends and family? It's funny. She has given me a home, a family, an identity, and a vision for my future and all I can do is to do good in school and care for my brother. But everything that goes around comes around, and blessings have been coming around for my mother for a while now - and I have no doubt they will keep coming.

It's been a pleasure writing the foreword for this book and with no further ado, I introduce you to my wonderful, amazing, awesome and amiable mother.

Miss Doobee Deborah Adura (Age 12).
Author of:
"The Two Princesses" *and several published poems, which include:*
"Pandemonium" *published in "Through Their Eyes: Verses from The UK Young Writers"*
"Hadestown" *Published in "Hunted: Mini Sagas from the UK"*
"Sacrifices" *Published in "Superhero Adventures: Southern Tales"*

REVIEWS

The book *Saved by Grace* is an interesting read for any Christian as it demonstrates the power of God. The book includes numerous real-life stories, including that of the author and it is an educational text about African traditions utilising the Tiv culture as a case study.

Saved by Grace serves as an inspiration to those who are going through a similar ordeal, whilst encouraging well-meaning members of society to intervene.

Dr Shadrach Kohol Iornem
Director programme at the London graduate school, President of Tiv Association in the United Kingdom.
(MUTUK).

The book *Saved By Grace* by Lois Hembadoon Adura discusses discrimination against the female child in African culture. In this book the author shares her personal story of suffering as a result of this discrimination and explains the need for male and female children to be valued in equal proportion.

Anyone who has been looked down upon or experienced rejection due to their gender will find this book inspirational, as it encourages success through determination and hard work. Indeed, it is a story of one who has been saved by the grace of God. 'God's grace cannot be disgraced by man's misguided cultural practices.' Therefore, I invite us all to share from the author's participant experience in life and learn how best to believe in ourselves and rely on God's grace.

Mathew Terhemba Kyoosu
Seminarian, Ilorin Diocese, Nigeria.

"All human beings, regardless of gender, should be treated with dignity and respect." The book *Saved By Grace* by Lois Hembadoon Adura, exposes female inequality in its basest form. Through both her own and other women's experiences growing up under the cultural practices of Tiv land, Nigeria, the author lays bare the lack of dignity and respect afforded to the girl child in this African region.

Yet despite the disturbing topic being exposed within its pages, this book is powerful and uplifting, praising the Lord for all that it is possible to achieve in life through the power of His grace, and with determination and self-belief. *Saved By Grace* is a battle cry for women everywhere, encouraging them to find the strength within to change their destiny and those of women around them.

"Praise the Lord. God has not made a mistake by creating women. We are unique and precious in His eyes. See yourselves as such."

Lisa Timms
Our Lady of Peace Parish, Burnham, UK.

ACKNOWLEDGEMENT

I would like to acknowledge God Almighty for the privilege given to me by His divine mercy to be able to write this book and narrate the ordeals, hardship and struggles of the female child in a society where the male child is overwhelmingly preferred. It can only be the amazing grace of God that helped a wretch like me succeed and come this far. With God's divine assistance, I have come to a realisation that all things are possible. There have been times in my life that I didn't have much confidence or believe that I could succeed at anything. However, with God in control, I know that no goal is too lofty, especially when you have Jesus as the centre of your life. Things get even better when one has a very encouraging, God-fearing, understanding and highly educated husband such as mine, Dr. Peter Terfa Adura, who sees the best in you and eagerly invests in your development. I am indeed grateful to you, my husband of 17 years, for all your unyielding love and support. To our two adorable and divinely favoured children, Doobee Deborah Adura and Sefa Samuel Adura, I owe you more than my limited vocabulary allows me to express at the moment. You are simply the centre of our universe!

It takes a big cast to support the stories that make up this book. Some of the stories are quite emotional and disturbing, and the happy-ever-after endings of the stories are fascinating. This book isn't written about the lives of just a few female children, whether their stories appear in this book or not. Each female child out there is in a similar situation, and I want to acknowledge how special you are, and to say *courage dear sister, courage!*

To those of you who have helped shape the stories and the process of getting these stories down on paper, I say a big thank you for your contributions. I see evidence of your life stories in this book, and most importantly, in my life. Your contribution in making this book a success has helped me tremendously and I know that, together, we will achieve the long-overdue justice and fair treatment for the female child in our society.

Thank you to my supportive, amazing, wonderful and amiable mother, Mama Pheobe Nyieyange Gbaa. You have been my pillar of support, prayer warrior, and motivator through-out my earthly journey. Your innumerable sacrifices to raise your children by yourself (as a widow) have made me a success story today. May God bless and keep you alive with us for the longest time. I pray to God to continue provi-ding us with the resources needed to take care of you in your old age. I owe you my unconditional love. Mama, God has wiped away your tears from the years of incessant disgrace and ridicule in a society that accords very little status to widows, never mind one without a male child.

It would be remiss of me to fail to acknowledge the enormous contributions and roles of several individuals in my life thus far, and most profoundly, my late uncle, Mr. Natheniel Gbaa, who sponsored my education. I am also appreciative of great, close family members (the Orkuugh Gbaa Abelaga, Bokpa Atanyi, and the

Adura families). I also have wonderful friends, mentors and spiritual fathers who have supported me massively over the years. Thank you.

My sincere appreciation goes to my knowledgeable spiritual father, divine brother, mentor and inspirer, Rev. Father Emmanuel Okami. You are such a wonderful mentor, my intercessor, my spiritual defender, editor and a precious brother indeed. This project would not be a reality without your inspiration and support. There were times when the task felt overwhelming but your constant uplifting words provided the extra energy that I needed. God knows the depth of my gratitude to you. Thank you so much.

My special thanks to my three siblings, Joyce Ngufan Asuku, Doom Stella Atetan and Sekegh Susan Gbaa, and their amazing children. You have been there for me with your continuous prayers, love and support. I also thank God for my wonderful friends whom I refer to as "sisters from different mothers", namely Mrs. Juliet Mchivir Wombo, Mrs. Miriam Member Senwua, Charity Loko, Mrs. Colleen Hembe Gbue, and Aisha Nwankwo. I couldn't have asked for better any better friends. Your prayers, spiritual and moral support have yielded fruit. May God bless you in trillion-folds. A big 'thank you' also to my sister-in-law, Mavis Hembadoon Adura-Ojiji for your love and support. You are a difference-maker.

My special appreciation goes to a special family - my God-given family, **His Royal Majesty, Orchivirgh Prof. James I. Ayatse-the Begha u Tiv, and his wife, Her Royal Majesty, Dr. Felicia Hembadoon Ayatse the Queen Mother of Tiv land**. Your special love, and support mean a lot to me. You are very kind for treating me as your blood relation.

Many thanks to my senior brother from another mother, Dr. Terver Agega and his family, for being a friend and a big brother to me indeed. May God bless you. Many thanks also to one who helped edit this book, my brother, Prof. Joseph Terzungwe Zume, and his wife, Mrs. Erdoo Zume who is a personal friend.

My sincere appreciation to my very wonderful aunties, Mrs. Florence Mvendaga Akighir, Mrs. Mwuese Abunku and my dear mother Mrs. Regina Akume for facilitating my relocation to the United Kingdom for greener pastures. With a grateful heart, I say thank you from the bottom of my heart for the uncommon opportunity you all gave me. God bless you all with your families. A huge thank you to my Sefa's Godmother, Jackie Lang and her family. You are a friend indeed. And a big thank also to Sefa's God father, Engr. Sylvester Jijingi. I also wish to express my gratitude to my son Dr Angus Torkuma Jijingi as well for being a son indeed to me.

A very special "Thank you" to the Akiga family - Late Mama Catherine Akiga, Chief Felix and Late Chief Mrs Martha Akiga, for welcoming me into your home when I needed a family in the UK, and for giving me the uncommon opportunity to meet my lovely husband in your house. May the souls of Mama Catherine and Mrs. Martha continue to rest peacefully with the Lord.

I will forever remain grateful to my personal motivator, son and mentor, Dr. Shadrach Kohol Iornem. He single-handedly talked me into believing that I could actually become an author. To further enhance my writing skills, he got me on his training program with the London Graduate School. He is my angel. A very big 'thank you' also to his team, Prof. Moti and Prof. David Iornem, for bringing out the hidden writing talent in me and making me an author.

A massive 'thank you' to my God-given family from Ghana: Sister Felicia Ellis, Brother George Ellis, and Brother Martin King, for their special love, support, generosity and for supporting me with my family so much. Your tremendous help is very much appreciated. Without your tireless support, this achievement would have been more laborious. God bless you.

These special brothers-in-law, Col. Joshua Asuku and Mr. Desmond Atetan deserve special acknowledgement. How could my story begin, or end without their unrelenting support?

My angel and daughter, Miss Doobee Adura! Isn't she very special? I don't know how I could have succeeded without her continued encouragement and inspiring words. She always sees the best in me and that has been a unique source of inspiration to me. As an author herself, she used her writing skills to proofread the manuscript of this book for accuracy. Thank you, my angel.

Finally, my deepest appreciation and eternal gratitude to my mother-in-law, Mama Beatrice Mbalamen Adura and my Late father-in-law, Papa Samuel Akaahule Adura for giving birth to my wonderful husband. You are the best; you are amazing parents. Thank you so much for being special and helpful to me, and for giving me your best treasure, and accepting me to be a part of your family.

DEDICATION

This book is dedicated to my glorious heavenly
Father, the Almighty God, the Creator of the
universe. He alone is worthy of my praise and glory,
for He has granted me the wisdom, strength,
boldness, divine directions and spiritual enablement
to write my first book.

To my outstanding and beloved husband,
Dr Peter Terfa Adura, who continues to be my
closest companion and soulmate.
I love you for just who you are.

To my precious children, Miss Doobee Deborah
Adura and Master Sefa Samuel Adura for been my
treasure, my joy and pride.
They are my unmerited gifts from God and the
reason I celebrate motherhood.

*To my late father, Papa Zachariah Ugber Orkuugh
Gbaa, your name is still alive in me.
To my late grandfather who always saw the best that
was in me, Pa Israel Orkuugh Gbaa Abelega.*

*To my wonderful mother, Mama Phoebe Nyiayange
Gbaa, for all your long suffering for us.
May you live long to enjoy the fruits of your labour.
You are my divine blessing and delight.*

*Finally, to all female children, orphans, widows,
barren women, women without a male child, and
women everywhere.*

CONTENTS

Foreword iii

Reviews vi

Acknowledgements ix

Dedication xvii

Preamble xxiii

Introduction 1

Chapter One:
GENDER INEQUALITY 29
- My question is: "Is this culture a
  blessing or a curse?" 31
- My early life struggles and my
  determination to go to school 32

Chapter Two:
A REVIEW OF REAL-LIFE STORIES 65
REAL LIFE TESTIMONIES OF
VICTIMS 79
- Due to a Disability I was Rejected
  as an Evil Female Child 85
- What crime did my mother commit? 89
- To err is human to forgive is divine 93

- The strength of a strong woman is unbelievable 96
- The wounds of this culture curse can be unbearable 98
- Sad ending for my mum 102
- I was punished as though I made myself to be barren 105
- True life story of a female struggle to go through education above all odds 106
- The male child syndrome 116
- My humble counsel to female children and womenfolk 119

Chapter Three:
TRIALS OF FEMALE INFERTILITY 123
- Society's Problems and the Girl Child 124
- The desperation of a tortured, humiliated and rejected woman 126
- My husband suffered infertility and died a broken man 140

Chapter Four:
IS THIS CULTURE A BLESSING OR CURSE? 143

Chapter Five:
BELIEVE IN YOURSELF 153
- Patriarchal tradition, women's vulnerabilities and disadvantages 154

Chapter Six:
SUCCESS IS ACHIEVED
THROUGH DETERMINATION
AND PERSEVERANCE 165

Chapter Seven:
TRIBUTES TO THE AUTHOR
FROM FRIENDS/FAMILY 171
- What is a tribute? 171
- Tribute by Dr Peter Terfa Adura
  (Author's husband) 172
- Tribute to an elder sister par
  excellence, my role model and my super
  woman with dimensional personality 173
- My big sister, my superhero, my
  mentor, my, mother and my role model 178
- My thoughts about my Auntie's life 180
- Tribute for Barrister Mrs Lois
  Hembadoon Adura 184
- A tribute to my mystery woman
  (An experience I will never forget) 191
- A diamond class friend 194
- Tribute from a friend and sister in Christ 196
- Tribute from a friend 201
- Tribute about my role model, mentor,
  big sister, inspirer and Big Mummy Lois ... 203
- My encounter with Mrs Lois
  Hembadoon Adura 206

- How I first met Mrs Lois
  Hembadoon Adura 211
- My encounter and meeting with
  Auntie Lois 215
- Tribute to Mrs Lois Hembadoon
  Adura (nee Gbaa) LLB, LLM, BL,
  AICMC, ICSAN 218
- Tribute from a learned colleague
  at Nigeria Law School, 2019 set 222
- Injustice against the girl child:
  A write up inspired by this book 223

Chapter Eight:
CONCLUSION 227
- My final counsel and notes to the
  girl child and women who had and
  are suffering from the paradox of
  unfavourable culture 230
- Recommendations and possible
  solutions to end male child syndrome 235
- An appeal to Our royal father:
  Your Royal Highness 237
- My honest Prayers for all female
  children, women with only daughters,
  widows, and barren women in Tiv land
  using myself as a point of contact 239

EPILOGUE 243

PREAMBLE

"Woe to those who make unjust laws, to those who issue oppressive decrees, to deprive the poor of their rights and withhold justice from the oppressed of my people, making widows their prey and robbing the fatherless. What will you do on the day of reckoning, when disaster comes from afar? To whom will you run for help? Where will you leave your riches?"
(Isaiah 10:1-3 NIV).

The overwhelming substance of this book is contextualized in view of the above Bible passage, which I encourage my readers to reflect upon as they read through the pages. In many cultures of Nigeria, and indeed, the entire Sub-Saharan Africa, the "male child syndrome" is endemic. Typically, a Nigerian father, irrespective of economic or social status, desires a male child such that, if they were to choose just one child, it would be a male.

Consequently, most women are in tears when they don't have a male child because of the fear of being ostracized from their families. Men often experience family pressures to have a male child to carry the family lineage. This contrasts sharply with the situation in the Western world where I reside presently. Here, some people on their own, might consider not to have children at all, or where they do, are perfectly content with just a daughter. Contrary to African countries, the female child in Western countries is cherished, highly adored, and respected. In Africa, a woman without a son to inherit landed properties and continue the family lineage could be thrown out of her husband's house. Ignorant husbands blame their wives for producing girls, and even those who are educated to know that a father's chromosomes determine the sex of a child, still blame their wives for giving birth to female children. In fact, for some families, a man starting out with daughters keeps bearing more children, sometimes taking multiple wives, until a male child is found.

Thus, the high fertility rates among African cultures is partly attributable to the pursuit of male children. The perceived relative benefits of male children as potential custodians of both identity and lineage have sustained this value over generations. **Is this culture a blessing or a curse?** A woman, who achieves recognition and status by the birth of at least one male child, is considered fulfilled and ultimately accorded greater respect relative to her counterparts who do not achieve the same feat. Studies have been focusing on the factors defining this gender preference at the expense of those that still sustain marriages that are "barren" - the tension and agony that characterize the psychological disposition of women in this dilemma.

While the subject matter is an African issue, the scope of this book is intentionally limited to my own cultural group - the **Tiv people of Benue State, in Central Nigeria, West Africa. Tiv culture is patrilineal,** and the practice of patriarchy among the group is so holistically implemented that mothers without sons appear to remain permanently relegated in the society.

The book narrates the ordeals, pains, and struggles of Tiv women who have only female children in their marriages and the derogatory status accorded them by their husbands, in-laws, and relatives who might be related to the husband in one way or the other. It also offers advice on how to improve things at the family, household level, and the community level as well.

INTRODUCTION

MALE CHILD PREFERENCE: A CULTURE THAT HAS A PREFERENCE OF SONS OVER DAUGHTERS.

You shall also say to the Israelites, "If a man dies, and has no son, then you shall pass his inheritance on to his daughter."
Numbers 27:8 (NRSV)

"The challenge of life is to change the circumstances of our birth into more personal and enjoyable ones and thenceforth to proceed into contented waning."
(Stewart Stafford)

First and foremost, I acknowledge and appreciate God Almighty tremendously for the grace He has granted me to write this book about my experience as a daughter growing up in a rural area in Tombo, Mbalagh in Tivland, Benue State, Nigeria in West Africa.

The ordeals, hardships, and struggles of a daughter and a widow with no male child in Tivland, where I hail from, cannot be emphasised enough. Such women can sometimes face discrimination and subordination in society. However, God's plans for us cannot be changed regardless of how society might have treated us as a female child; God determines our expected end. All women faced with these challenges need strength in the struggle, a strength that comes from God alone.

> 'I will strengthen you; I will help you; I will uphold you with my righteous right hand.' says the Lord of hosts.
> Isaiah 41:10

All human beings, regardless of gender, should be treated with respect and dignity. That is why Section 18 of the 1999 Nigeria constitution, dealing with the fundamental principles of state policy, reflects the nation's commitment to equality of all, irrespective of race, sex, or gender (Osokoya, 2008). However, Assimang (1990) noted that even though African Women have been making immense contributions to both family and national development, they still face a number of inequitable difficulties that limit their potential in promoting personal and collective wellbeing. To support this, research studies have pointed to inequality in the treatment meted out to infertile women.

In Tivland, women are singled out for blame in every marriage where infertility is a challenge, often without further medical investigation to ascertain where the problem lies in order to treat it. Many marriages have broken down as a result. Infertility is a problem that affects both sexes; it is not always women's problems that cause the lack of pregnancy. Men can also be deemed infertile as a result of many medical conditions, such as sperm disorder, hypogonadism, ejaculation disorder, and other underlying male medical problems.

This singling out of women as the issue happens because the Tiv people traditionally have a patriarchal structure, characterised by gender inequality. Patriarchy is defined as "a set of social relations with a material base that enables men to dominate women" (Okojie, 2001). It is a system of stratification and differentiation based on gender, which provides material advantages to males, whilst simultaneously placing severe constraints on the roles (childbearing) and activities of females. Patriarchy also conditions the spatial segregation of males and females, with the male space comprising the wider public domain while the female space consists largely of the insular household and its immediate environment. As a result, Tiv women are expected to marry early, reproduce, and care for their children. When they fail to produce children, the dominant male society turns against the women.

An infertile woman in Tivland stated:
"The problem with infertility is not that you have nobody to help you, but that society does not respect you. For a woman, respect is only due if she is the mother of children. Even young people do not respect you when you are not the mother of their mates" (Hollos, 2003:54).

I am narrowing my concerns to focus only on the Tiv community where I come from. While every parent-to-be wants a happy, healthy baby, many among the Tiv people cannot deny that they have a sex preference. In Nigeria today, many communities, including the Tiv community, have come to believe that if a woman has not delivered a baby boy, then she has yet to make an impact in the family.

The idea to write on the topic of male child syndrome was borne out of my own experience of growing up as a daughter without a father and a brother to protect me. It was also borne out of strength in the struggle of a village girl with a vision; a vision to break the ordeal, pains and the constraints put on her for being a girl, with very limited help from the people who believe in this culture that prefers sons over daughters.

Girls from backgrounds such as mine, but also women in Nigeria generally, face discrimination and subordination in society at large. The subordination of women is even more pronounced on daughters living with their widowed mothers and also women who have not produced a male child for their husbands. It can only have been God's amazing grace that helped a girl like me to succeed against all odds, after losing my father when I was six years old, and worst of all, being a girl with three sisters and an illiterate widowed mother, with no brother to protect us. My mother, Mama Nyieyange

Pheobe Ugber had only a small yam farm and a portion of land for rice farming as a source of livelihood. This livelihood was all she had to help raise our family, never mind sponsoring me to achieve my dreams.

To be honest, during those days, life seemed like a dead-end for my dreams. However, much later in my teenage years, I realised that all things are possible through Christ. I learned this Scripture through Sunday school classes in my local church (N.K.S.T Church Akulaga Tombo).

> **"I can do all things through Jesus Christ who gives me strength."**
>   **Philippians 4:13**

Through this Scripture, I was physically and spiritually lifted to pursue my dream, no matter what obstacles and challenges were in my way. The farm provided only for our food and basic needs; however, I resolved to help my mother in farming for our survival. But I was determined to go to school in the morning, come back and go to the farm in the evenings and at weekends.

Thank God, the State-owned primary schools were free in those days, otherwise I couldn't have afforded to attend primary school because my mother didn't have the money to pay. However, she only needed to buy one set of uniform and a few exercise books for me. I had no need for sandals and socks, nor for a backpack with textbooks and a lunch box, as these were considered a luxury for those who could afford them. I only needed slippers (flip-flops) to protect my tiny feet from walking barefoot in the scorching sun.

Although the State primary schools were free as mentioned previously, some of the teachers in the rural areas made going to school a bit hard, especially during the farming season when we were working on their farms most days. So, I gained very little knowledge due to the minimum teaching we received. This was worse for those of us who were girls and hardworking, as we were always the first to be picked from the classroom to go to the teacher's farm, or to fetch water from the stream (which was some distance away) for the teachers and their families.

Sometimes, we were asked to cook for their families, which would take almost half of the school day. You would cook the food without tasting it because you were not allowed, even though you might be hungry. Some teachers were very mean, and their wives were surly and mean. As a child, you would smell the sweet aroma of the food and salivate, but you would not be offered any of the food to eat.

As a child, it was so difficult for me to cope. Some days when I came back from school already exhausted, I would go to the farm in the evening to help my mother, or grind maize with a grinding stone to make flour for food for the family. Then, I would go to the stream to bathe with my siblings and fetch water for household use in large containers, weighing up to 20–30 kg, which we carried on our heads. I was doing all this before I was even ten years old.

Most parents preferred to keep their daughters away from school, to help them on the farm, but my mother loved the idea of me going to school, so she never made me stay at home to go to the farm with her in the mornings. Some parents had a belief that sending a girl to school was not a good idea, especially the illiterate ones. They believed that the girls would mingle with the boys and be violated or be corrupted in their manners. So, keeping them at home to farm with them was safer, and helped prepare the girls for an early marriage. So, for me, insisting on going to school was seen as being wild and seeking to be corrupted.

My mother's elder brother, with whom we were staying (having been sent away from our father's house because we were girls), did not believe in educating a girl, especially one like me without a father or nor a brother to protect me. He always said to my mother, 'My sister you don't have a child, and the only girls you have to prove you have a womb, you are allowing them to go to school to become corrupt?' None of his daughters went to school. Whenever my mother was not home for any reason, I would not be fed at the end of the day if I attended classes.

We had no support at all from him and his first wife, who had ten children. None of them went to school except for the last girl, Nguevese Aishi, who came to live with us. I brought her to live with us when she was three years old, after her mother's death. I enrolled her in primary school and paid her school fees through to the University level. She is the only educated one from my maternal uncle's family.

Staying with my maternal uncle was difficult. I was left at the mercy of my destiny helpers. Fortunately, his second wife, Mama Vandelun Aishi, had no children of her own, so we 'became her children'. She was the best mother we had, and my father's married half-sister who also lived in the village, Aunty Nguoon Gbaa – Aluga, became our saviour by secretly giving us food. We became very close to her and her children. She was an angel with a heart of gold, and absolutely the best aunty. She was so very kind and generous.

With all this trauma in my life, there were times when I did not have the confidence in myself to believe that I could succeed, especially living in this sort of environment, surrounded by people with mediocre mindsets. It was very difficult to dream big and then to live your dream. However, through my faith in God, fervent prayer life, determination and perseverance, I have come to realise that no goal is too lofty to achieve, especially when Jesus Christ is the solid rock on which you stand.

> **"The Lord is my rock and my fortress and my deliverer, my God, my rock, in**

whom I take refuge, my shield, and the
horn of my salvation, my stronghold."
Psalm 18:2

Those were some of the Scriptures that gave me
the hope that I can do all things if I make Jesus
Christ the Lord of my life, my rock, and fortress.
I am so glad that I took the bold decision to
accept Him as my personal Lord and Saviour
and decided at a very tender age, to follow Him
for the rest of my life with no turning back. I
embraced Jesus with all my heart, and I continue
to do so.

In the African culture, especially where I come
from, the Tiv community in Benue state,
Nigeria, the struggle of a girl who is determined
to succeed by depending on extended family
members and family friends for assistance can be
a very big challenge, especially without a father
figure. Your destiny, though designed by God, is
largely in the hands of your helpers and that's
only if you are lucky enough to get someone who
is willing to accommodate and sponsor you
through education, alongside their own
children. Be very grateful and appreciate these
helpers. However, although some will help, they
will abuse you a lot.

Being a girl from a poor background in the quest to be educated through the sponsorship of wealthier family members can sometimes cause you a lot of pain. One of my colleagues narrated her own experience growing up with her paternal uncle. She said that her father had only two children, no boys. She wanted to go to school, and so she was sent to stay with her uncle in the city who took her virginity when she was just eight years old and continued to sexually abuse her. Between the ages of thirteen and fifteen, the uncle, who was a doctor, carried out two abortions on her at his clinic.

Sometimes her uncle's abuse hurt her so badly that she struggled to walk properly or do any domestic work and his wife's physical abuse made her frequently run back to her parents in the village. Her aunt was very inconsiderate, and even though she had told her aunt what her husband was doing, she denied that her husband could not do such a thing and accused her of sleeping with boys at school.

To make matters worse, each time she ran home to her parents, her father would insist on taking her back, with a stern warning not to mention her ordeal to anyone as it would bring shame and disgrace to the entire family. He didn't want people to know that his younger brother was sexually abusing his daughter.

The main underlying factor here was that her uncle was their source of income and the breadwinner in the family. So, it was deemed that this that gave him the right to violate his niece's fundamental human rights. Her uncle physically and mentally abused his niece for years in the name of sponsoring her through school, until she became of age and ran away with her friend. She had confided in her friend and her friend's mother offered her shelter and sponsorship to University level; she is now a lawyer. Her father is still alive and maintains that the issue should not be reopened in order to cover up family shame.

Another big obstacle, aside from the one already mentioned, was growing up with those so-called family members. Some could turn you into a slave and punching bag on a daily basis, but others were extremely kind and generous, and treated you as one of their very own children. Some were nice but this came with a huge dose of maltreatment and the expectation that you would be grateful for the favour they were offering by accommodating and sponsoring you. This made staying with family members for sponsorship a painful experience on a daily basis.

I have experienced the good, the bad and the ugly. However, God does not allow His own to suffer forever. When you are going through a tough time, you can sometimes feel like your strength is fading away. You can become tired and weary of hoping for change. Your faith begins to waver. It's in these times that I advise you of the need to draw closer to God. This advice might feel like the last thing you want to hear, especially if you are wondering why God hasn't brought you out of the struggle yet, but trust me, this is the best thing you can do in tough times. You will definitely come out of whatever challenges that you face; you will definitely come out of it victorious and much stronger, because it is God who can provide the strength you need to keep going until you see a breakthrough.

I am living proof of God's awesome grace. His grace found me through my immediate uncle (my father's elder brother, Late Mr. Nathaniel Nder Gbaa), who offered to sponsor me after primary school. He was a wealthy man, and owned Savannah Printing Press Ltd in Jos, Plateau state.

He sent one of his half-brothers (my half-uncle, Mr. Jack Dyako Gbaa) to come and get me from Tombo Mbajembe, the village where I was staying with our maternal family, along with my mother and siblings, to take me to N.K.S.T Secondary School, Zaki-Biam, where I started my schooling. This was a drastic change in my circumstances overnight and this is how my life transformation started. I glorify God immensely for that wonderful opportunity and an open door for me to achieve what has become my success story.

God is awesome. The Bible tells us many times that God is our strength. The psalmist wrote:

> **"God is our refuge and strength, a very present help in trouble."**
> **Psalm 46:1.**

God's strength is something we are promised; He says: 'I will strengthen you; I will help you.' When we feel overwhelmed by the circumstances in our lives, we can go to God and find rest.

He hears our prayers and also the cry of the helpless.

Hallelujah... the hour and day I dreamt of had finally come and I was overwhelmed with the joy of my new opportunity. From that day forward, my uncle took me into his home during school holidays, treated me as his daughter, provided for me and sponsored me through my secondary education to advanced levels.

He never maltreated me, and his first wife Late Mrs Elizabeth Ajiryila Gbaa was an angel in human form; may her precious soul continue to rest in peace with the Lord. She was a mother with a golden heart to all of us under her care. His second wife, Late Mrs Comfort Ngunan Gbaa, who married my uncle after the death of his first wife, was a good aunt as well. They treated me very kindly and gave me more than I needed. I gave my excess to my mother and siblings. My cousins used to give me lots of their very expensive fairly used clothes, shoes, bags, textbooks and everything a girl needed.

I used to cook in the kitchen by myself and eat with the family at the dining table as part of the family, which was a luxury most of my friends who were also growing up with relatives didn't have. I must confess that through that training, I am a very great cook indeed and an extremely tidy person.

I had my own beautiful room, which was well furnished. The family had housemaids, gardeners, gate men and drivers, so I didn't have to do any hard work at all. Most of my friends in secondary school and College of Education thought my parents were rich, as most people that knew me at this time thought I was my uncle's biological daughter. I owe my late uncle my sincere appreciation forever. He was my superhero. I love you and will forever miss you dad.

Unfortunately, my happy story was the opposite to that of some of my friends, who were brought up by surly and mean family members. Their lives staying with those relatives in the city were daily torture, going to bed late on an empty stomach, being maltreated, and going to school with holes in their shoes and uniforms.

St. Paul said:
"We were crushed and overwhelmed beyond our ability to endure, and we

thought we would never live through it. In fact, we expected to die. But as a result, we stopped relying on ourselves and learned to rely only on God. And he did rescue us. We have placed our confidence in him, and he will continue to rescue us."

2 Corinthians 1:8-10

Thank God they survived the hardship; some are well established in life now, because they did not give up on their dreams, but rather took their suffering as an opportunity to succeed at all costs. We talk about our experiences and laugh about it. It's all history now.

These are just some of the limitations the societal negative influence has against girls with a bright future. Most girls have potential, however not many of them with potential for greatness become great in life. This is because there are enemies of distinction that prevent them from becoming what they are meant to become; the great enemy called societal influence. Girls face discrimination and subordination in different ways, with it forgotten that they are the future of the society; they are the future wives, mothers, daughters, sisters, aunties and the nutritional bedrock of human society, who feed and nurture mankind and at the same time manage the home. Despite this, girls continue to suffer subordination, and the ability to fully realise their potential is greatly hampered.

This book is intended to be an eye-opener to families in Africa, especially among Nigerian communities who practice this harsh culture, and to encourage them to abolish it and give girls equal educational opportunities. Investing in a girl's education is beneficial to the entire community. This book also intends to serve as a campaign to create awareness on the importance of both boys and girls.

My book is an encouragement to extended family members who have the resources to help their less privileged family members, to please help those who cannot afford to go to school due to lack of sponsorship, regardless of their gender. Some may appreciate it, and some may not, however, help them anyway. In doing so, together we will conquer poverty and positively expand the dreams of others. Girls - appreciate those who are sacrificing things to sponsor you through education. They are God sent; show them gratitude, please.

I was **"saved by grace"** through the generosity of family members who sacrificed to make me who I am today. For this, I try in my own little way to be a bridge for other victims to succeed. As a beneficiary of others' kindness, I do my best to assist those who are willing to go to school because this is the least I can give back to the community I benefited from. I feel strongly that I need to do something to help female children within patriarchal societies, to be their advocate in one way or another.

My success story cannot be told without talking of those people who saw the best in me and held me up and I stood tall. My gratitude goes to some specific people who I will mention as I tell my story; their acts of kindness cannot be taken for granted. This is my way of saying thank you to them a million times, because without them, surviving with my mother and siblings (now Mrs Joyce Ngufan Asuku, Mrs Stella Doom Atetan and Ms Susan Sekegh Gbaa) would have been even more difficult.

We were pulled through life by the kind acts of these 'Good Samaritans' and the amazing grace of God. It wasn't easy at all; however, God was in total control and therefore we can humbly say that we are survivors to the glory of God. We all face adversity, and challenges at some point in life, don't we? Unfortunately, some of us remain trapped in this adversity and our lives end there. Our case was different.

My daily prayer is "Lord, I am so grateful to you for seeing me and my sisters through it all, growing up as girls with no father or brother to speak for us. However, Jesus, you were always there and have always been there for us. We say thank you Jesus a million times."

I want to take the opportunity through this book, to speak directly to the heart of that girl who is almost giving up on her dream. Right now, you are thinking there is no hope, because help is not forthcoming from any corner. My book aims to bring you hope, so that you can turn your adversity into opportunity by refusing to give up. I use myself as a reference point to encourage you today that all hope is not yet lost; keep believing and trusting God. Keep being good and trust in the Lord with all your heart;

your destiny helpers are closer than you think. It is never too late. If I made it, you will as well. Don't give up. God's plans for you are for good, not for evil. They are plans to give you an expected end.

> **"For I know the plans I have for you, declares the Lord, plans to prosper you and not to harm you, plans to give you hope and a future."**
>
> **Jeremiah 29:11.**

When you read this book, tap into God's amazing grace and it will give you a motivation to dream big and pursue your dream, even when there seems to be no way or hope. Dare to trust God. Be positive; turn all the negative situations in your life that are meant to break you, into steppingstones to climb up and achieve your dreams. Keep reminding yourself that even if the enemy of your progress means evil, God will turn it to your advantage.

> **"Even though you intended to do harm to me, God intended it for good, in order to preserve numerous people, as he is doing today."**
>
> **Genesis 50:20.**

This book is intended to be a motivational and inspirational book with the objective of exposing and condemning the mentality and common belief in our culture that places more importance on the boy over the girl. I condemn it in its totality. All children are blessings from God and must be treated equally.

I wish to encourage all girls to be determined not to accept this culture and settle for less. Whatever a boy can do, a girl can do better. I am a living testimony. I defied all odds and broke the belief that a girl is only good for marriage, not for education and having a career. I instilled this positive thinking in my younger sisters when we were all young; it was important for them to think highly of themselves and never allow a boy to intimidate them. This was our only defensive strategy for survival in a boy's world.

I now tell my daughter this as well.

"This is the true joy of life, the being used for a purpose recognised by yourself as a mighty one, the being a force of nature instead of a feverish, selfish little clod of animals and grievances complaining that the world will not devote

itself to making you happy. I am of the opinion that my life belongs to the whole community, and as long as I live, it is my privilege to do whatever I can. I want to be thoroughly used up when I die, for the harder I work the more I live. I rejoice in life for its own sake, life is no brief candle to me. It is a sort of splendid torch which I have got hold of for the moment, and I want to make it burn as brightly as possible before handing it on to future generations."

George Bernard Shaw.

African parents, love your children equally regardless of gender. Daughters are gifts from God as well. We bear your names as well, and when we succeed, the credit goes to you, our parents, just like the boys. Stop putting limits on your daughters. Abolish this culture and give your daughters the same opportunities that you give your sons.

THE SCOPE AND STRUCTURE OF THE BOOK

Chapter One:

This chapter provides a general background of the Tiv traditional culture, its patriarchal structure and the pains, ordeals and struggles of girls. I narrate my early life experience of surviving without a father or brother, the betrayal of family who were meant to be our protection, the struggle through primary school and my determination to continue my education at all cost.

Chapter Two:

This chapter narrates life stories of women who grew up under this harsh culture that preferences boys over girls, the abuses they went through, and their determination to break the limit placed on girls. Their narratives cover their ordeal, hardships, and struggles growing up as girls with limited opportunities, and show their survival strategies and how they have risen to achieve success regardless, along with their messages of encouragement to other young women.

Chapter Three:
This chapter tells the story of women who have been tortured, humiliated and rejected for their inability to bear male children, along with the effect male child syndrome has on women. However, some of those women are more than determined to make their daughters succeed, regardless of their hardships and some have broken this cultural curse over their daughters to ensure they are successful. This was my mother's belief as a woman who had suffered rejection, emotional and mental torture as a consequence of not having a son for her late husband.

Chapter Four:
Is this culture a blessing or a curse? Should we all fold our arms and accept this African tradition of gender inequality between males and females? Or is it high time women speak out about the difficulties of life and the fate of girls trying to succeed amidst this patriarchal structure? This chapter narrates the girls' battle, which starts from the day they are born through to the day they die. From birth, teenage years, maturity and married life - the battle is endless. How can women survive through all these

phases and be successful, without continually being hurt?

Chapter Five:
Believe in yourself; do not conform to the patriarchal tradition. This chapter emphasises the vulnerabilities and disadvantages women are exposed to in the patriarchal tradition: the pains women go through to survive and make a career. Being a rejected female child or a widow/wife rejected for your inability to bear a male child doesn't hinder God's purpose for your life from being accomplished. God can do so much more than you can even imagine.

Chapter Six:
Determination and perseverance guarantee success. Defy all odds to achieve success by being a prayer warrior. Stay connected to God and watch how He will conquer your battles for you.

Chapter Seven:
This chapter will be dedicated to testimonies of family and friends about the author, how they know her and their relationship with her, and a tribute about the author.

Chapter Eight:

The concluding chapter contains the author's final words, recommendations and key encouragement notes, with strong prayer points for parents to love both their children equally regardless of sex.

1

GENDER INEQUALITY

PAINS, ORDEALS, AND STRUGGLES OF FEMALES AMONGST MALE DOMINATED SOCIETY

> *"Do not be conformed to this world, but be transformed by the renewing of your minds, so that you may discern what is the will of God—what is good and acceptable and perfect."*
> *Romans 12:2*

Generally, African traditions have a patriarchal structure characterised by gender inequality between males and females. Okojie (2001), defined patriarchy as "a set of social relations with a material base that enables men to dominate women." As mentioned previously, it is a system that is classified into different groups and these groups are differentiated based on gender, providing material advantages to males whilst simultaneously placing severe constraints on the roles and activities of females.

This system also conditions the spatial segregation of males and females in society; the male space consisting of the public domain, whilst the female space consists largely of the household and its immediate environment. Thus, in this male-dominated system, women's activities are largely confined to the household. In this way, African women are expected to get married early, bear children and take care of them. When they fail to bear these children, the male-dominated society ill-treats them, and they're left to bear the painful ordeals of the patriarchal system they find themselves in.

Traditionally, Nigeria is a male-dominated society. Notwithstanding, women have made a tremendous impact in the lives of the so-called male personalities. The major problems women face in society today are as a result of what had already started on the home front.

Women who give birth to only female children are perceived by this culture as unproductive women. It is even worse if the woman is widowed and has no son. She is considered a curse and the reason why the late husband died without a male child to succeed him and keep up his family lineage. In some families, the widow is thrown out of her husband's house, and if the husband has assets, she is thrown out empty-handed. Family members either take everything and share this among themselves or one male member of the family takes it for himself and his family. No one reproaches them about this inhuman treatment towards the widow and her daughters. Sadly, this is what most widows go through in some communities in Nigeria, including Benue State, where I come from, although this harsh treatment differs from family to family.

My question is: "Is this culture a blessing or a curse?"

Tiv women face different barriers, deep prejudice, and discrimination daily. Most men argue that the reason they prefer a son is so that the family name can be sustained, the son can inherit property, and it meets the need to conform to the wider culture and traditional setting. These statements baffle me because they show the ignorance of these men who are otherwise educated, articulate, and career-driven, but yet have this mediocre mindset.

The male child syndrome is a depressing issue. What is so important about the male child anyway? In the society in which we live today, women are also doing very well and, in some cases, even sometimes better than some men. Many women are the breadwinners in their household. I became a breadwinner for my mother and siblings at a very young age through hard labour. I am also aware of bad-mannered male children who are only good for carrying out evil deeds in their families. So, what is this the whole noise about a "male child"?

My early life struggles and my determination to go to school

"For we are what he has made us, created in Christ Jesus for good works, which God prepared beforehand to be our way of life".

Ephesians 2:10

My late father had two elder brothers and two elder sisters. My father was the last child, and I was told he lost his mother while she was giving birth to him. My father died when I was only six years old and I am my father's first daughter.

I am narrating my ordeal in good faith; not with bitterness, but to seek a purification of this culture. I do love all the people who treated me badly. I have forgiven them from the depth of my heart. They trained me with love in a hard way. I would do anything in my reach to help any of them or their children.

"Do not withhold good from those to whom it is due when it is in your power to act."

Proverb 3:27

They might have meant evil, however God turned it to my advantage. It was ignorance and the culture that made some of them behave the way they did. I've learnt life's lessons the hard way, and I am very grateful to God for His amazing grace that has saved a wretch like me. All these hardships have drawn me closer to God and given me compassion, and as a result I love people unconditionally and I'm willing to help as much as I can.

I am a victim of this sad cultural curse and belief. Growing up as a girl, I heard this phrase so many times, ***"you are just a girl or prostitute."*** After my father went to be with the Lord, my mother did not have a male child, and so my father's older sister, who as my aunt was supposed to protect me, would always accuse my mother of being the reason why her late brother died without a son.

She hated me so much because I was a girl, even though a woman herself. She had two daughters and one son. That one son who is no better than her daughters in any way, made her think she had a better social standing than my mother. She despised me and my sisters so much and she didn't hide it.

At every contact she had with me, she would say very irritating things to remind me that I was a girl and worthless. She would always call me names, horrible names.

After my father's demise, the incessant verbal abuse and ill-treatment from my uncle became unbearable. This didn't bother my mother; she remained in her late husband's house until my uncle asked her to leave since her husband was no more. He took the farm my mother had as her only source of livelihood and gave it to his last wife. He was heartless enough to throw his own late brother's wife and children out on the street. I have forgiven him as he is my blood. I love him and treat him with the respect and integrity given to a father. There has been some expression of remorse on his part in recent years. He even asked my mother to take her farm back after over forty years of surviving without it.

After we left, we still had some contact with my paternal family and visited now and again during my primary and secondary school days. There were a few times during those visits, when my aunt would be so mean to me, verbally and physically abusing me on several occasions. On one particular occasion, we visited to attend a funeral. I was eating with my cousins when she came in and dragged me away from the food.

What had I done to deserve that kind of treatment? It was simple – I was a girl! My father's other sister was there watching and confronted her on why she treated me that way. The great news in all this is that I had truly forgiven her from the bottom of my heart before she died. I don't blame her, however, it's sad that I never had any close relationship with her. I have forgiven her because she acted in ignorance because of the cultural curse laid on a female child, which was the only culture she knew. We cannot blame her; she didn't know any better. She allowed her zeal for her culture to get the better of her morals, even though she was a woman and had daughters.

There were several instances when, for no just cause, I was maltreated and insulted. When I was a teenager, I was talking with my cousins and I said, I wanted to become a lawyer when I grew up in order to defend the cause of the girl child. One of my older cousins said mockingly, "Who will dash you, you think to be a lawyer is prostitution?" (I was a virgin at that time, so how did I become a prostitute?) He shouted at me and told me to leave the group that was talking. That was mean. I cried so much that day, however, I forgave him because he was very narrow-minded.

On another occasion, one of my father's half-brothers pushed me into the deep part of the river. We lived close to the river and from time to time we used to go to the riverbank as children. I was about to drown when out of the blue, another half-brother of my father appeared and saved me. He dived into the river just in time, as I had gone under the water. When he brought me out of the river, I was bloated; he then pressed my stomach and water came out of my mouth, ears, and nose. That was how I was saved from drowning.

Life was hard without a brother to protect me. All this happened to me because my crime was being a girl without a father or a brother. He wouldn't have done this to his own sisters.

I thank God for such mean relatives, because they trained me the hard way, and I am grateful to God that I turned out strong and brave.

Sadly, this poor behaviour is even perpetrated by women against their own gender. They who should be their sisters' keepers, instead turn out to be the ones who make a mockery of their female counterparts. Some women in the family used to create quarrels with my mother just for the opportunity to remind her of her inability to have a son. It was heart-breaking; she had to live with the insults as though she had made herself not have a son. Sad, isn't it?

However, to every sad story, there is a happy ending. We are victorious and united in love; Jesus is for us. We have conquered and proved the bad ones wrong. Girl power wins. Most of these family members are still alive to witness God's amazing grace upon me and my siblings. I say this humbly with no arrogance intended, but with sincere humility.

Those women who had sons and thought they had made a name for themselves and felt they had hit the jackpot, where are their sons now? What can those sons do that we girls cannot do? What have they achieved that we girls haven't? What benefits do they bring home to their mothers that we girls have not given to our mothers? Where have they travelled to that our mothers haven't? Are they living a better life than our mothers? Have their sons brought them a new life or built houses for them, that is better than our mothers'?

The answer is a simple no. Some of them are living in very pitiful conditions, surrounded by their sons. None of them wants to be reminded of all the ordeals they put us through now. Some will read this book with so much bitterness in their hearts and will say, "How dare she?" But I am being honest.

Once, my grandfather (Late Pa Israel Orkuugh Gbaa) called almost all his daughters who were present on that day, to his sitting room. Out of all his granddaughters, he invited only me to this meeting. He then began to pronounce blessings upon me in front of his daughters. This infuriated my aunt and she protested and cried out loud saying, "What an insult, I am your firstborn, how dare you choose to bless a granddaughter over me or my children?" She made a big show of that and wanted her sister and half-sisters to protest with her. However, no one else saw anything wrong with my grandfather's actions, even though they were not blessed like me, except for her. After my grandfather died, I travelled abroad and didn't visit Nigeria until 2009, when I went home for my traditional marriage. This same mean aunt of mine had no other good words for me. She said; "Your grandfather chose to give all his blessings to you, and this is why you are prospering; so, go and pour lager beer on his grave and thank him!" My other aunt rebuked her and said, "Why can't you be happy for this girl for once." I laughed and walked away.

Our God is merciful. He can send destiny helpers to you from where you least expect them. He came forth for us through other kind-hearted family members, who helped us tremendously.

We cannot ever repay them for their acts of kindness to us; all we can say is a huge thank you, with a sincere prayer to God for them and their families.

We are saved by God's amazing grace to all be alive today to testify of His goodness and mercy upon our lives and our families. We are grateful to all of you that made sacrifices to help us during our wilderness days.

Our most profound gratitude goes to Late Aunty Nderamo Leke, Aunty Felicia Shiwua Gbaa, Aunty Nguoon Aluga, Aunty Deeyem Dzever,

Aunty Shimekem Iordzenda, Aunty Bee Aondoakaa, Aunty Kasevbee Chigh, Aunty Nguyan Nyiuma, and Aunty Avaa Ueng.

These are my super squad of aunties, all who saw the best in me. God bless you all. I love you all very much.

I love this song and have made it my comfort song:

AMAZING GRACE
John Newton

Amazing grace! How sweet the sound
that saved a wretch like me!
I once was lost, but now am found;
was blind, but now I see.

'Twas grace that taught my heart to fear
and grace my fears relieved;
how precious did that grace appear
the hour I first believed.

Through many dangers, toils, and snares,
I have already come;
'tis grace hath brought me safe thus far,
and grace will lead me home.

The Lord has promised good to me,
his word my hope secures;
he will my shield and portion be,
as long as life endures.

Yea, when this flesh and heart shall fail,
And Mortal life shall cease,
I shall possess, within the veil,
a life of joy and peace.

The earth shall soon dissolve like snow,
the sun forbear to shine;
but God, who called me here below,
will be forever mine.

When we've been there ten thousand years,
bright shining as the sun,
we've no less days to sing God's praise
than when we'd first begun.

I learned the words of this song whilst at secondary school as a member of the Fellowship of Christian Students (FCS). This song became my comfort song, and I would sing it whenever I started feeling frustrated and thought of giving up. I would sing it and believe the words. When I read the life story of the author of Amazing

Grace, I began to see my life as being saved by grace.

So, I decided within myself not to give up, but to use my experience to reach out to every girl out there who is giving up on their dreams due to the circumstances surrounding them, to tell them to please not give up. Nothing good comes easily, but help is on the way. God is mindful of you and your plight. He miraculously delivered Newton from the horrendous storm off the coast of Ireland and He has delivered me and my siblings. He is still the same God. Trust Him with all your heart, and refuse to see your circumstance as a hindrance, rather see it as a steppingstone to achieving your dream.

"Trust in the Lord with all your heart and lean not on your own understanding; in all your ways submit to Him, and He will make your paths straight".
Proverb 3:5-6.

Your story is not different from mine nor Newton's, nor some of the ladies who have shared their experiences in this book. These are real stories of how God's amazing grace can save. If I survived by determination and bravery, growing up in those harsh conditions and a culture that placed so much importance on a son over a daughter, then you too can be saved by His amazing grace.

If you are reading this book and thinking this whole culture curse is not true, it is real and not a myth. The most worrying aspect of this belief is the fact that a female growing up in a biased world of male preference has very little support. The culture curse puts so much constraint on daughters. A daughter is denied so many opportunities to explore her talents and creative ability and to succeed in the community.

Unfortunately, this trend has taken a turn for the worse, as some men now use it as an excuse to take second wives, and they then produce children that they cannot take care of. I know of a family that wanted only three children but kept on having more children in the name of having a male child and ended up having ten girls and still being without a male child. To be honest, it is only an ignorant man that will blame his wife for having daughters, because women do not determine the sex of a child, God does.

It is high time men realised that they determine and supply the Y chromosome that produces the male child, so they should stop blaming their wives. Some gullible women are out there waiting to wreck their fellow women's marriages in the name of manufacturing male children - as though they are God.

Women, be careful how you ruin other women's marriages; karma may come back to haunt you and you may experience the same issues. Whatever you sow, you will reap. This preferencing has caused trouble in so many families, as the men end up having illegitimate children and these 'male children' end up becoming a nuisance and disappointment to the family and society in general.

My honest advice to great women out there who have been affected by this evil culture, is do not kill yourselves trying to have a male child at all costs. We are not God who gives life, so be content with what you have. Women are indeed faced with too much trouble in the home to allow such trivial issues to bother us. A child is a child, no matter the sex. It is not about the sex but about the personality and what that child will be and will offer society that matters.

This wrong mentality has destroyed many homes and made many more poverty-ridden. We ought to be counting our blessings rather than making selections, for there are many out there that are praying to just be able to have a child, regardless of sex.

Disregard this culture because it puts so much burden on women and their daughters. I became an adult at a very tender age to support my widowed mother and my three sisters to prove the culture wrong. I needed to be strong for my mother and stood up to defend my sisters. But how many girls out there have this determined spirit to fight for their rights?

My grandfather used to say to me, "My grand-daughter, even though you are a girl physically, you are actually a boy on the inside." He was a wise old man who had foreseen my bravery and fighting spirit. He knew I was going to succeed in the world of males, because of this fighting spirit to survive and achieve my dream.

In every tunnel there is always light at the end. Help came along.

"I am about to do a new thing; now it springs forth; do you not perceive it? I will make a way in the wilderness and rivers in the desert."

Isaiah 43:19

Where there's a will, there's a way. Even in the most difficult situation, God is faithful. God will make a way out of no way. This was my firm belief, and truly, God did. My destiny helper showed up.

My father's elder brother, Mr. N.N. Gbaa was the best, and he gave me the uncommon opportunity that has made me who I am today. As I told you earlier, he offered to sponsor me from secondary school to A level (College of Education). This was an opportunity I had wanted so much and getting it was divine and I never have nor ever will take it for granted. He was my God-sent, and the best father figure I could have had. I am forever grateful to my late uncle.

He was extremely generous, kind, loving and my superhero; a real definition of a father and an uncle par excellence. I love you, rest in peace.

Just when I thought all was well, suddenly things took a U-turn. When I got admission to the University, I went to tell my sponsor and ask him to assist me again. However, he told me in a very calm and polite manner, "My daughter I would have loved to, but I am sorry, you have to struggle on your own now. I am compelled to do this; my hands are tied. I hope you will understand me my daughter."

This was because a member of his immediate family had told him to stop wasting his money on me and so, that was the end of the sponsorship. However, I appreciated him greatly and told him politely with tears in my eyes not to worry and that he had done his best to support me. I won't blame him. I accepted my fate in good faith and thanked him for all he had done for me already and left. I thought that was the end of my education. However, as I left his house, I said to myself, "Be more determined than ever, this is just the beginning of my adventure, all hopes are not lost for me."

I continued with my petty businesses (I was selling second-hand clothes, firewood, and small supplies in Benue Cement at that time) and in training my sisters. God blessed me a lot through this business. I did not have much money, but we were in search of greener pastures compared to other very poor families around us. Most families around where we were living used to look up to me and cited me as a good example to their daughters.

I was involved a lot in my local church activities and doing charity work to help the less privileged in my community. I was helping those I could within my reach. At this point, my uncle's decision gave me a boost to achieve my educational dream at any cost. I knew he was pressured to take that decision, but he was a good man.

Shortly after that, I relocated to Abuja to settle there in search of a greener pastures. I enrolled back to school for a distance learning course with the Federal Polytechnic Ugbokolo, for an Advanced Diploma in "Public Administration." The idea was to study and run my petty business at the same time. I completed that course and then concentrated on paying school fees through to university level for my three sisters, before I continued my education again. It was my desire for all of us to be educated to university level. This was the only way we would get a good standing in a society dominated by males.

Whilst doing all that, another challenge arose. I didn't want to get married, even though I was of marital age (I was in my middle twenties). I resolved that I would marry when the time was right, and the right man came along. This issue attracted many insults from family members, even the educated ones. Some family members took it personally and called me all sorts of names. But I refused to give in to pressure and kept doing what would benefit me and my siblings and God remained with us. It was an education I wanted, and miracles do happen. God has helped me to achieve my academic dream with an LLB and LLM (Master of Laws in International and Commercial Law Policy, International Oil and Gas Specialist) at His appointed time.

Two of my sisters are also degree holders, while the last one is a holder of an HND.

One with God is the majority. I give Him glory and honour for being so faithful to us. It's never too late with God on your side. Who would have thought I would achieve this much? I am a product of grace - a girl from humble beginnings, who fought to turn her life into a success story: a story that I pray will act as encouragement for many girls who are going through a similar ordeal.

Don't give up, be more determined.

We are all **saved by grace** and this grace of God is sufficient to save you as well. However, the path to success can be extremely difficult and challenging for girls with a vision to succeed in life, living within this sort of environment. Even if they have positive affirmations, they can be easily misled into not believing in the possibility of their dream and then decide not to pursue it. They end up settling for less, thinking they are not good enough. They live with the prejudiced lies and mediocre mindset of 'I am just a girl; therefore, I cannot amount to anything.' Don't be brainwashed by those lies. You are unique, valuable, beautiful, and stronger than you can imagine.

My strong advice to girls in this kind of situation is that the power of decision is very important. I made up my mind and took a firm decision from my teenage years to succeed regardless of my gender and the negative environment that was against me as a female child. I used to question God sometimes, to prove Himself to me - if He was real, let Him pour His grace upon me and lift me out of my predicament so that one day I could tell my story to encourage other daughters like me. For this reason, I refused to give up and settle for mediocrity.

I fought a good fight for my equal right to go to school and be what I wanted to be in the future. I refused to give up, not even the culture could stop me or put a limitation on me and my siblings. We were called names and faced a lot of rejection, but all that happened so that our success story would be a breath-taking one. Not every girl who went through what I did survived it and came out stronger, but I did and so can you. There is still hope for other girls coming behind us, but we must put a stop to this culture.

I was a different African girl with a different spirit, a Joshua and Caleb kind of spirit, who believed that though the giant may be in our way to hinder, God would surely give us victory. I refused to be limited nor labelled. I am who I am; unique, knowledgeable, creative, beautiful, intelligent, adorable. Thank God my mother is alive today to testify to the goodness of the Lord and His amazing grace that has saved a wretch like her and her children. One with God is the majority.

I remember vividly one day when I was sleeping in my room, and around midnight, I had a dream. In the dream I was asleep but felt a tap on my foot to wake up, which I did and in the dream, I saw a man holding a paper with a Scripture boldly written on it: **Proverbs 23: 25.** I woke suddenly from my sleep and quickly opened my Bible to read that particular Scripture passage to see what was written there, and this is what it says:

> **"May your father and mother rejoice;
> may she who gave you birth be joyful."**

From that night, I knew God's plans for me were not to fail but succeed regardless of what we were going through. I believed that Scripture so much and held onto it and started reciting other Scriptures about God's amazing plans for my life.

> **"For I know the plans I have for you,
> declares the Lord, plans to prosper you**

and not to harm you, plans to give you hope and a future".

Jeremiah 29:11.

However, even though I knew God had promised good to me, things did not change automatically, and the struggle continued. Some days I felt like giving up, but I had siblings looking up to me, so I couldn't afford to lose hope, and we had come too far. There were a couple of temptations that got me whilst trying to survive as a girl. My experience is that people can use your vulnerability to abuse you before they offer any favour to you. However, in all these trials, Christ was my ultimate goal and focus, so I never lost track of my faith. I would turn to Him at all points in my life, despite my shortcomings.

I never lost hold of my faith, though from time to time I would backslide due to human nature. But I was a very active member of my local church (NKST Church), as the girls' youth leader for years, a Girls Brigade member all my life, GB Officer, and a choir member, and I knew I was a sinner and needed Jesus to cleanse me.

Therefore, my faith was very important to me. I made up my mind from my early childhood days that the culture would not limit me and my sisters. I own my life and therefore, I can do all things through Christ who strengthens me, and I refused to be defined and limited by a man-made culture that is biased. If God is for me who can be against me, except myself. Therefore, I chose to make the Word of God my reference point and a guide for my life to succeed. I am who God says I am; therefore, no culture can separate me from the love of God and His plans for my life. My destiny is in God's hands.

"Who shall separate us from the love of Christ? Shall trouble or hardship or persecution or famine or nakedness or danger or sword? As it is written: 'For your sake, we face death all day long, we are considered as sheep to be slaughtered.' No, in all these things we are more than conquerors through him who loved us. For I am convinced that neither death nor life, neither angels nor demons, neither the present nor the future, nor any powers, neither height nor depth, nor anything else in all creation, will be able to separate us from

the love of God that is in Christ Jesus
our Lord."

Romans 8:35-39

I started using positive affirmations to be the
architect of my life by declaring words such as:

> **"I am the architect of my life;**
>
> **I build its foundation and choose its
> contents.**
>
> **I am brimming with energy and
> overflowing with joy.**
>
> **My body is healthy;
> my mind is brilliant; my soul is
> tranquil.**
>
> **I am superior to negative thoughts
> and low actions".**

I refused to give up. My sisters and I were going
to prove to the culture that the stone the
builders rejected shall become the cornerstone.

> "Jesus saith unto them, did ye never
> read in the scriptures, the stone which
> the builders rejected, the same is
> become the head of the corner: this is

the Lord's doing, and it is marvellous in
our eyes."

Matthew 21:42

Through all these difficulties I came to
understand the value of positive affirmations, as
they are simple by nature, but their effect can be
very powerful. Repeating and believing in the
words you speak is healing, and positive
affirmations can help release you from
negativity, anxiety, fear, and a whole lot more. I
am where I am now because I refused to look
down on myself, and when all the people around
me and my community were saying there is a
casting down in a girl child, I was saying there
was a lifting up for me and my siblings in Jesus
name.

I recommend that all girls/women use positive
affirmation, especially those of you reading this
book thinking that your life will not change no
matter how much you think positively. That's
not true, that's a lie of the devil; do not believe
it. Your life will change if you decide to change
your negative thinking. Positive affirmations are
phrases (thoughts) that you repeat to yourself,
which express a specific outcome that you seek

to bring to reality. For example, "I am good enough, smart enough and worthy enough."

Initially, these positive affirmations will probably not make sense or sound true in your mind. When you want to bring about a positive change in yourself, it generally means you don't believe yourself to have that desired outcome/mindset, etc. However, by not just repeating positive affirmations, but believing them to be real, you change your thoughts for the better and that then becomes your reality.

Seriously, positive affirmation works; like magic. When I used to talk and declare boldly what I wanted to be, most family members used to mock me and say, "Who does she think she is? You are just a girl. You won't amount to anything other than prostitution or marrying and bearing children". Those statements used to hurt so much. Ignorance is a killer disease. No wonder the Scripture talks about lack of knowledge destroying a community:

> "My people are destroyed for lack of knowledge: because thou hast rejected knowledge, I will also reject thee, that thou shalt be no priest to me: seeing

thou hast forgotten the law of thy God,
I will also forget thy children."

Hosea 4:6

It's unbelievable how human beings put limitations on others and say mean words to others to cause them pain, without knowing the extent of the damage their careless words can have on another person.

In 2002, my aunty and her husband (Mr Simon and Mrs Florence Mvendaga Akighir) who lived in the UK, invited me to come over for a better life. Our lovely aunty (Mrs Mwuese Abunku) who was in a position of authority through the honourable office of our dear mother in Israel (Mrs Regina Akume) helped facilitate the process. I got the visa to come to the UK and with excitement and great joy, I went to share the good news with one of my paternal uncles, with my immediate younger sister's husband (Col. Joshua Asuku) and my childhood friend's mother (Late Mrs Orban). On getting there, my uncle listened to me as I shared the great news. He thought for a while and responded thus; "Why do you want to go abroad Hembadoon? Instead of you considering settling down in Nigeria to marry and start a family, you want to go abroad and do prostitution?" My jaw dropped, my brother in law's countenance changed in disbelief at what had just come out of my uncle's mouth. My childhood friend's mother broke down in tears and asked that we better leave immediately. I laughed, because I was used to hearing such words, as they had been used on me ever since I was a little girl. So, to me, it wasn't a big deal. It didn't bother me anymore.

To me, marriage was not just about me being old enough to get married, it was about waiting for God's time, and waiting for my perfect husband. I wanted a man who would be a father to me, a brother, a soulmate, a companion, a friend indeed; a man who would not bring back the past pains of my childhood by abusing me or reminding me that he was more superior than me. A God-fearing man was my ideal husband; a man who would support me in achieving my dreams. A man who would see the best in me when all odds were against me. A man with a poor background like me who would understand and appreciate God as we made our life together. A man who would accept my mother and siblings. A man who would make his family my own. A man whose family would accept me as their own.

Within six months of my arrival in the UK, I met the man of my dreams through his God sent mother (Late Mama Catherine K. Akiga). She introduced my husband to me. Mama, my angel, rest in peace. I love her so much and she will forever occupy the best part of my life. She was extremely kind to me and loved me as her biological daughter. My husband is not just a husband, he is an angel in a human form; a rare breed, my greatest supporter, and inspirer, the brains behind my success. He is a complete gentleman with very unique qualities, an outstanding personality and he is the best husband in the whole wide world (BHITWWW).

About two years ago, one of my junior uncles (my grandfather had so many wives that some of my uncles are younger than me) was insulting a very prominent Tiv son on social media; a personality above him, a man who is very much older than him and far better than him. I reproached him saying, "My brother, using such strong language against an adult on social media is not acceptable." He ignorantly replied and said, "Self-appointed lady, whatever you are in the society, you are just a girl in our family; you will not be seen as anything to me because you are just a girl."

I said, "Hold on, what I said to you has nothing to do with being a female or male, it was about having good morals." Although he is literate, he has an illiterate mentality. He forgot the fact that success is not measured by being a man. It is measured by your hard work, determination, and achievements.

Success has no hashtag of strictly a 'male affair'; there is no such thing like that in life. You achieve it regardless of gender.

Come to think of it, is there any door a man will enter, and I won't be allowed to enter because I am a woman? No. There are only a few limited doors you can enter strictly by merit and your achievement, which I am privileged as a woman to go through. Success is not a man's right; it is a choice, and I chose success. I am the architect of my life; the traditional culture cannot put a limitation on me. My success depends on God. It's sad that some of my family still nurse these ugly feelings against me.

"Limitations live only in our minds. But if we use our imaginations, our possibilities become limitless."

(James Paolinetti)

I always remind myself that I am a strong woman because I have dealt with almost everything that has hit me in life. I have cried myself to sleep, picked myself back up and wiped my own tears. Life has knocked me down a few times through friends and family who have made themselves available as agents to be used by the devil. They showed me things I never wanted to see: the good, the bad, and the ugly sides of life. I have experienced sadness, rejection, name-calling, blackmail, false accusations, judgement and failures. I always get up and promise not to take revenge because vengeance belongs to the Lord. As my Baptismal verse from Romans 12:21 (NIV) says:

"Do not be overcome by evil but overcome evil with good."

I have grown from things meant to break me. I get stronger by the day and I have God to thank for that. I don't sit around feeling sorry for myself, nor do I let people mistreat me. I don't respond to people who dictate to me or try to bring me down nor do I allow any factor to limit me. If I fall, I will rise even stronger because I am a survivor and not a victim. I am in control of my life and there is nothing I can't achieve, because I can do all things through Jesus Christ who strengthens me.

I believe in being strong when everything seems to be going wrong. I believe that happy girls are the prettiest girls. I believe that tomorrow is another day, and I believe in miracles. I am a living testimony of this, a drastic miracle myself. All I have ever achieved is purely by grace and the miracles of God in my life.

I am saved by grace.

2

A REVIEW OF REAL-LIFE STORIES

> *"You don't develop courage by being happy in your relationships every day. You develop it by surviving difficult times and challenging adversity".*

"Do not those who plot evil go astray? But those who plan what is good find love and faithfulness." Proverbs 14:22

To those who use culture to disadvantage one gender over another for their advantage, be warned as the scripture above has clearly stated.

In this chapter, I will be narrating sad stories African culture can cause the female children and women in some parts of Nigerian culture. To understand the phenomenon of "culture", it will be better to give an in-depth analysis of what it is and its implications.

According to the Cambridge Dictionary, culture is defined as "the way of life, especially the general customs and beliefs, of a particular group of people at a particular time."

The American Dictionary says; "Culture is defined as the way of life of a particular people, especially as shown in their ordinary behaviour and habits, their attitudes towards each other, and their moral and religious beliefs."

Merriam-Webster also defines culture as "the customary beliefs, social forms, and material traits of a racial, religious, or social group", and also as "the characteristic features of everyday existence such as diversions or a way of life shared by people in a place or time", and further explains culture as "the set of shared attitudes, values, goals, and practices that characterizes an institution or organisation".

Culture is the characteristics and knowledge of a particular group of people, encompassing language, religion, cuisine, social habits, music, and arts. The Centre for Advanced Research on Language Acquisition goes a step further in defining Culture as shared patterns of behaviours and interactions, cognitive constructs, and understanding that are learned by socialisation. Thus, it can be seen as the growth of a group identity fostered by social patterns unique to the group.

There is a paper presented on the Cultural Globalisation in Africa, with a particular focus on Nigeria, entitled "Is Culture a Curse or a Blessing?" It was written by Professor Gbenga Fakuade, from the department of Linguistics and Nigerian languages, at the University of Ilorin.

According to the Professor, "Culture constitutes the prime pattern and gradation of goods or values which people experience from their earliest years, and in terms of which they interpret their developing relations. Young people peer out at the world through lenses formed, as it were, by their family and culture and configured according to the pattern of choices made by that community throughout its history (Mclean, 2006). Thus, through time, culture builds and nurtures tradition or heritage."

He goes on to illustrate the concept of culture as a complex concept that incorporates the combination of a people's beliefs, knowledge, and tradition. It defines a group of people living in a certain area of the globe or people who share a type of heritage. Culture is something that belongs to one because of birth. It refers to everything from what they eat, whom they pray to, how they dance, what type of music they make, their social habits, their dresses, their superstitions, their sets of values, and their language.

According to Tylor (1871), culture is that complex whole which includes knowledge, beliefs, art, morals, law, custom and any other capabilities and habits acquired by man as a member of society. According to De Rossi (2017), culture encompasses religion, food, what we wear, how we wear it, our language, marriage, music, what we believe is right or wrong, how we sit at the table, how we greet visitors, how we behave with loved ones and a million other things.

As diverse as all these definitions of culture are, many of them emphasise similar things, and because of this, culture has been defined "as the complex whole of a society" - this definition can include everything that gives a society its identity. It has also been noted that cultures share at least, five basic characteristics: they are learned, shared, based on symbols, integrated, and dynamic (cf. Nowaczyk, 2016). At this juncture, one may ask whether culture and tradition are the same. The terms culture and tradition are generalized terms that are often used interchangeably because it is easy to believe that they are coreferential. However, there are distinct differences between them, despite similarity and overlapping.

Tradition has been described as the set of customs and beliefs that are passed down the generations in society and still practised by the people of a society. Courtesy (2014) argues that if beliefs and behaviours have been forwarded from one generation to another, it qualifies to be described as a tradition, whereas, culture reflects the beliefs and ways of life that differentiate one society or community from another. Thus, traditions and culture play a major role in the identification of a particular society: they are therefore society or community bound.

Through all the definitions and in-depth clarification of what culture really is, the big question that needs to be addressed remains: "Is culture a blessing or a curse?"

Based on the above definitions, I believe that culture is supposed to be a blessing not a curse, because it gives a group of people in a particular community an identity. Why then do some certain communities in Africa, especially among communities in Nigeria in particular, misuse their culture to disadvantage a particular gender over another in the name of tradition?

Is this what culture really means? Why make the culture structure to favour some and punish others? Are both genders not all human beings? Are all children not a blessing from above? Why can't parents celebrate both children equally?

Do women determine the sex of their children? Why is the heart of some people desperately wicked and greedy? It is only God that can save mankind by His divine grace because the heart of the human person is desperately wicked.

The Bible is very explicit about those who make these unjust cultures:

> "Woe to those who make unjust laws, to those who issue oppressive decrees, to deprive the poor of their rights and withhold justice from the oppressed of my people, making widows their prey and robbing the fatherless. What will you do on the day of reckoning, when disaster comes from afar? To whom will you run for help? Where will you leave your riches? Nothing will remain but to cringe among the captives or fall among the slain. Yet for all this, his anger is not turned away, his hand is still upraised".
> **Isaiah 10:11**

Loving your neighbour is a command:

> "Hearing that Jesus had silenced the Sadducees, the Pharisees got together. One of them, an expert in the law, tested him with this question: "Teacher,

which is the greatest commandment in the Law?" Jesus replied: Love the Lord your God with all your heart and with all your soul and with all your mind. This is the first and greatest commandment. And the second is like it: Love your neighbour as yourself. All the Law and the Prophets hang on these two commandments".

Matthew 22:34-40

This is the first and the most important commandment: love your God and your fellow human beings as you love yourself. Does this culture show the kind of love Jesus emphasized in the Gospel? The definition of culture includes our religious practice as well. So, if we are so zealous about practising our so-called culture, why not practise all that the culture entails? Remember we are all saved by grace; be kind to one another, and do not ever allow a man-made culture to compel you to commit evil against your children. All children are blessings from above.

The phenomenon of male child preference is not new. It has in fact existed for centuries. Females have suffered degradation and dehumanisation through the ages. However, this differs from community to community and family to family.

It is rare to hear about women leaving their husbands as a result of their infertility. They would rather protect their husbands and take the blame for infertility. I have a friend whose husband had an infertility problem, and she has protected him and taken the blame for 22 years of their marriage. The husband's family members fought her and insisted the man send her away without knowing he was the cause of their childlessness. She was determined to stand by him even though she was the breadwinner of the house. The man was the one that told me his predicament and asked me to help him appreciate his wife and to commend her for standing by him all those years. He said he couldn't share his problem with any of his family members as they wouldn't understand nor believe him. They would mock him and say that he was protecting the wife since she earns more than he does, but that wasn't the case.

When I spoke with the wife, she broke down in tears and told me how she had been carrying the secret for years and had promised to be faithful to God and her husband 'til eternity. She had hidden it from her family as well because they would have insisted that she leave her husband. Just a year ago, the husband had some fertility treatment and to cut the long story short they now have a boy and a girl.

Would any man sacrifice this much for his wife? I don't think so. But why not? Marriage is a total package, and you cannot pick and choose which aspect of the package to accept and which one not to accept.

I think a good marriage and happiness in marriage are created by both parties regardless of children. I read an online article about a good marriage, written by Wilfred Arlan Peterson. Peterson's view on a happy marriage is:

> "*Happiness in marriage is not something that just happens.*
> *A good marriage must be created. In marriage, the little things are the big things.*
> *It is never being too old to hold hands.*
> *It is remembering to say "I love you" at least once a day. It is never going to sleep angry.*
> *It is at no time taking the other for granted; the courtship should not end with the*

honeymoon; it should continue through the years.

It is having a mutual sense of values and common objectives.

It is standing together facing the world. It is forming a circle of love that gathers the whole family.

It is doing things for each other, not in the attitude of duty or sacrifice, but the spirit of joy.

It is speaking words of appreciation and demonstrating gratitude in thoughtful ways.

It is not looking for perfection in each other. It is cultivating flexibility, patience, understanding, and a sense of humour.

It is having the capacity to forgive and forget. It is giving each other an atmosphere in which each can grow old.

It is a common search for the good and the beautiful.

It is establishing a relationship in which independence is equal, dependence is mutual, and the obligation is reciprocal.

It is not only marrying the right partner, not only having male children; it is being the right partner and managing your challenges together".

Husbands, stop being selfish and respect your wives' feelings. Have some empathy for your wives. Going through infertility issues alone without your husband's support can be very depressing. Men, do not give the devil a footstool to step into your marriage and destroy the beautiful love story you have shared over the years!

Miracles still happen. Be patient, **I got married at 34 years, had my first child at 39 years and the second child at 46 years and I conceived naturally, when the doctors told me I had less than 5% chance of ever becoming pregnant according to the doctors' reports. I had no eggs.**

My God differed the report of the doctors and gave me two beautiful children, a girl, and a boy. This happened because my husband was super-supportive all through. **I had five ectopic pregnancy miscarriages with five surgical operations and almost lost my life**; however, God preserved me for the purpose of sharing my testimony and encouraging other families who are struggling with the issue of childbearing. I advise that you wait for the Lord. Please take heart and wait for the Lord. His timing is the best. This is my testimony; however, read below about some fascinating stories of female children survivors. Some of the stories will leave you speechless, but they are truth and captured in this book as encouragement to many reading this book.

Below are some of the success stories of female children who survived the degradation and dehumanisation of being a female child in a culture that preferred male over female children. These are true stories, not fiction. Some of these emotional stories I have captured in this book ended well; however, how about those who have not been able to pull through their ordeal? Some have lost loved ones in this battle while some are still in the captivity of this culture. Women are going through a lot even as I write this book, and there are underlying causes driving this. Something needs to change. An amendment of this culture is demanded by the few survivors on behalf of those still suffering.

All names and details have been withheld to avoid the individual being stigmatized. People have told their stories in the hope that they will help others who are being abused through this evil culture. I do hope that **our Royal father The Tor Tiv Prof James Ayatse** will read our stories and abolish this long-standing culture or help create an awareness among his Traditional chiefs to help eliminate the mentality of **"do or die affairs to have a male child."**

It's my sincere prayer that the stories in this book will encourage someone never to give up on their dream. Though it might seem that He tarries, God will surely show up at the right time with His divine mercy. We are saved by His amazing grace.

Please fathers, be kind to your wives and female children; we desire dignity and respect. God takes joy in seeing His children happy. Though weeping may last throughout the night, joy comes in the morning.

> **"God never said that the journey would be easy, but He did say that the arrival would be worthwhile."**
> **Max Lucado**

REAL LIFE TESTIMONIES OF VICTIMS

My afflictions

Growing up as the first girl child who lost her father in a motor accident, leaving his widow behind with five girls, was the biggest emotional challenge I went through. Having to cope with the sudden death of my dad was one thing; thinking of how we were going to survive with our mum without any source of income was another burden. Thinking of how we were going to continue school without sponsorship was what I dreaded most, and the reality was not pleasant.

To cut the long story short, we were living in Lagos with our Dad who had a very good job with an oil company, and life was very beautiful. Our dad didn't allow our mum to work since we were very comfortable with his job. However, the unexpected happened when he was coming back from work and had an accident; he died at the scene. We were devastated by the news of his death. Mum went into a coma for days before she recovered to face the reality of what was

waiting for us. As soon as she regained cons-
ciousness, and even before our father's burial,
the family members came from Benue and told
mum that they had come down to Lagos to pack
their brother's stuff to take home. As the first
child, I asked, "Which home? This is our home;
we have not known any other home. We barely
visit Benue State."

However, they moved everything from our
house into the truck that was waiting outside.
Their reasoning was that their brother died
without a child, because we were girls. Our mum
told us to remain quiet and not to argue with
our uncles and to let them pack whatever they
wanted. The most precious thing in her life had
gone, so she didn't need to fight over material
things while her husband's body was still in the
mortuary.

They packed virtually everything, including our
personal belongings. They said even our
personal belongings were bought with their
brother's money. That's how our ordeal started.
Our dad was buried afterwards, and then the day
after the burial, my Dad's younger brother asked
to take my mum; tradition demanded that he
inherited his brother's property which included

taking my mum as his third wife! This was someone who could not afford to look after his children; it was our dad who took care of their upkeep. My mum said over her dead body and ordered us to go inside and start packing, saying that we were going back to Lagos the same day.

Unfortunately, on returning to Lagos, an even worse ordeal was waiting for us. My mum discovered our dad had willed our house in Lagos and that he also had a son we did not know about from a mistress. That meant every one of his benefits belonged to the brother we didn't know about. So, we ended up with absolutely nothing to survive on, not even the house in Lagos and we had to move out of the house for our so-called half-brother to move in, with the support of our dad's family members.

Our poor mum accepted her ordeal, and we moved into a one-bedroom apartment with the money she had in her savings account and started petty trading with a provision shop. We were all withdrawn from our schools, as they were expensive, and she could not afford our school fees anymore. We were moved into local government schools, but even then, paying school fees was a struggle for our mum every term. Most of our dad's friends we turned to for help began to make advances towards us and so we stopped going to them for help.

At one point, I was contemplating following my friend's lifestyle and advice to start dating "sugar daddies" for survival, but I refused and kept my faith. I was determined to break my limits to achieve my dreams at all costs regardless of our circumstances. We had the basic things we needed, so that was enough for me. I used to encourage my sisters to stay strong for our mum. Mum brought us up in the fear of the Lord and we were all dedicated believers, all lovers of Jesus, and very active in our local church. Help came at last after years of torture, hunger, real suffering. I graduated with a first-class degree and served with an oil company and they retained me because of my hard work and integrity. Jesus made a way where there seemed to be no way. As far as I am concerned, suffering for us is history. Most of those my uncles are still alive, still very wretched and sadly my half-brother is living a worrisome life. He couldn't go to school as drugs took the best of him. All my sisters are graduates with very good jobs. Our mum dedicated her life to serve God and she never remarried.

I wish somebody could do something about this inhumane culture of preferring a male child over a female child. It has been my desire to put our story down in writing but never got around to do it. I am so proud that another female child with a similar experience decided to write about this evil culture and condemn it.

My advice to other girls out there is to not give up; although the giant called culture may be a sad hindrance, God will surely give us victory. Many are the afflictions of the righteous, but the Lord delivers us from it all. Don't give up, keep the faith, be determined and persevere. Success awaits you. My four sisters and I have used our girl power to defeat the evil culture curse of undermining a female child and you can as well. Be strong; you are not alone; we have the willpower to win.

The Bible says:
> **"Anyone who belongs to Christ has become a new person. The old life is gone; a new life has begun!"**
> **2 Corinthians 5:17**

So, once you are in Christ Jesus, the culture has no hold on your destiny.

Each day we face three enemies: sin, Satan, and ourselves. Our old self still wants us to believe the culture curse can stop us. Ignore those thoughts and do not believe in them. We know the culture is biased and wrong but if we do not allow it to break us down, it does not have a strong hold on us. The enemy uses this so-called culture to attack us and try to lead us down the wrong paths, but we can overcome these cultures by living the crucified life.

St. Paul wrote: *"I have been crucified with Christ; it is no longer I who live, but Christ lives in me."* What does it mean to live the crucified life? It means we let Jesus take over the running of our lives and we surrender our desires and goals and let Him give us better ones.

We walk in His ways rather than the cultural belief. Living Jesus' way isn't easy. We have to keep surrendering, sometimes moment by moment. But living His way is worth it because His way has no limit pressed on us for being female children. We have His power in us and He can work through us.

Even if we're struggling in our walk with Him, we can be grateful that His death on the cross means that we're acceptable to God and welcomed into His presence. When we mess up, He forgives us. When we walk away, He welcomes us back.

However, challenging it seems, let's pick up our cross and surrender to God. We are female children who have been "Saved by Grace."

Anonymous

Due to a Disability I was Rejected as an Evil Female Child

My father is a very wealthy man with lots of companies all over Nigeria. He married my mother and had two children (girls). I was the second and was born with a severe disability. I was crippled from birth and I couldn't walk until I was twelve years old. I was called an evil child, and my dad left me to survive or die at the mercy of my maternal grandmother who was extremely nice to me. She nursed me and looked after me very well. Even though my dad is a millionaire, I couldn't get the benefit of going to school because he said I was an evil child.

My mum was sent away and my dad remarried. My stepmother didn't want to hear my name, never mind talk of me going to their house to see my dad and ask for a favour. I lived as an orphan. Fortunately for me, where I was staying with my grandmother, another elderly woman there saw that I was a destiny child and continued to pray for me and encouraged me. She would always tell me that I would walk and encouraged me to believe in my heart that it would happen.

One day, out of the blue, I stood up and started learning how to walk. She celebrated me as though I were her own biological child. She would hold me up to support me to walk a few steps every day, until my legs became stronger and I could stand on my own and walk for a bit. She kept encouraging me to be strong and determined to walk. God perfected my healing and I started walking, however, I had some other challenges to contend with. I never developed breasts and I had not started menstruating.

My grandmother helped me by sponsoring me in school to secondary school level. After that, God sent my destiny helper, my lovely husband who proposed to marry me regardless of knowing my situation, as I didn't hide my disability from him. I give God the glory; our marriage is blessed with four beautiful kids. Despite the culture that labelled me as evil because of my disability and because I was a female child, I am now a spirit-filled woman full of joy and appreciation to God. "I am Saved by Grace." To crown it all God sent a man of God who has secured me a great job. Isn't God awesome? One with God is a majority. I give God the glory.

My advice to all female children out there struggling with this cultural belief and thinking that there is no way out, is that there is light at the end of every tunnel. Don't give up and remember that all girl children are beautiful. They are blessings from God, priceless gifts. We do not need the approval of men to succeed, regardless of our gender.

God is for us, we will conquer. Don't give up, keep being strong, your time to shine is around the corner.

One unique thing about all this persecution is that when we have an assignment from God, Satan will repeatedly attack us and try to stop us from fulfilling it. I was born a unique female child to fulfil God's purpose and the enemy knew, so he used the culture to attack me and labelled me as an evil child. Always remember these things about Satan's attacks:

1. His attacks reveal that he believes we're capable of accomplishing our goals. If he didn't think we'd achieve things from God, he wouldn't try and stop us. It shows that we're strong and full of faith. If we fall, he wants to keep us down because he knows if we rise again, we'll be stronger and more effective than ever.

2. He always attacks the start of something significant in our lives. The enemy tried to stop Jesus just before He started His ministry by tempting Him in the wilderness (you can read about it in **Matthew 4:1-12**).

3. We might feel more of an attack when we're just about to get started on something we are passionate about, or just before God gives us the next thing He wants us to do.

4. He uses those closest to us to reach our hearts. He can work through others to cause us to doubt ourselves and our calling. Other people

can make us feel insecure about who we are, and what we can achieve. We should never forget that our attitude is more important than the attacks we are experiencing **(Hebrews 12:15)**. Our influence in God's kingdom determines the level of attack the enemy launches against us. So, if we're facing a big attack like this culture curse about female children, let's not be discouraged but instead be encouraged by the fact that we're making a big difference in society.

Anonymous

What crime did my mother commit?

The question I keep asking is, what crime did my mother commit by giving birth to a female child? I hate telling my story; however, I have to share it to encourage that girl child out there who is going through rejection and insults of all sorts because she is a girl, and not a boy.

My mother got married to my Dad after they graduated from the same university together as medical doctors. Their marriage was blessed by having me, but unfortunately, I came out as a girl, so my dad's joy was not complete. He loved me and gave me the best education, but he was not satisfied having me as his only child. Maybe if I was a boy, he would have been content with what God gave him. However, his attitude changed towards my mum and he started keeping late nights. My mum, being a God-fearing woman, tried to hide all this from me and go through this alone. I started noticing my dad's late-night outings and sometimes coming home drunk. My mum would welcome him and hurriedly take him inside to shower.

I was a kid but not I was not stupid. I noticed those changes and asked my mum questions.

I sometimes confronted my dad, but my mum would stop me from talking to my dad like that. This carried on until one fateful day my dad's elder brother came from the village and called my mum and dad for a meeting. He then told my mum that she does not have a child with his brother, only a girl and so, the family had made the decision that my dad should take a second wife who would come and bear him a male child.

My mum was less than 35 years old, and there was a possibility that she could still get pregnant at some point, but my father's family members were impatient. My mum agreed with their decision without confiding in me. A few months later, the second wife was brought into our house, and the atmosphere changed. My mum was limited to certain areas in the house and the second wife took charge of the house my mum had helped my dad to build. She conceived and had a boy, and then my dad asked my mum to move to the servant's quarters, as his new wife needed more space to raise the boy. My mum, not wanting any trouble, moved to the boy's quarters, however, the second wife was not satisfied and asked that my mum be moved out of the house as she feared that her son was in danger with my mum around.

My dad obliged this request and moved us out of our home to another house. My mum's brother rejected the idea and gave my mum a better place for us to stay. We moved to my uncle's house, and he changed the house document and gave the house to my mother as a gift. My mum brought me up single-handedly and gave me a decent upbringing in the fear of the Lord.

> "Train up a child in the way he should
> go, and when he is old, he will not
> depart from it."
>
> Proverbs 22:6

I am, by His grace, a medical doctor and married with two children now, a girl and a boy. My husband treats our children equally. My mum is a very happy grandmother, with a kind-hearted son in law.

Sadly, later on, my dad discovered that the two boys he had with his second wife were not even his biological children. Only their girl was his biological child. The shock and anger broke him, and he got hypertension which resulted in a stroke. My mum took him into her house, nursed and cared for him 'til he passed away.

The estranged wife sold our house and married the father of her two boys. The girl, who was my father's child, is with my mum living very happily. It wasn't her fault that her mother was evil so we can't blame her, and after all, she is my blood. She calls my mum her real mother and is a good girl. Where were my uncles when my dad was in dire need of help on his dying bed? None of them showed up! It was only my mum, me, my husband and our children who were there for him. This is a big lesson for all those parents who put preference on their children's sex.

Anonymous

To err is human to forgive is divine

I have forgiven all my uncles. The benefit of forgiveness is that you are also free. Forgiving others is essential for spiritual growth. My experience of forgiving my uncles who had hurt me was painful, but come to think of it, it is liberating. Thoughts of resentment, anger, and hatred represent slow, debilitating energies that will disempower you if you continue to let these thoughts occupy space in your head. If you could release them, you would know more peace. More so, we need to forgive so that we are forgiven by God. Jesus' blood is the only way for this to happen. We must humble ourselves and forgive others to receive forgiveness. My story is a good teaching for those who are struggling to understand forgiveness.

Are you forgiven? Your eternal future depends on the answer to this serious question. The Bible teaches us that *"There is none righteous, no, not one."* (**Romans 3:10**) Verse 23 of the same chapter states, *"for all have sinned, and come short of the glory of God."* We must find God's forgiveness if we want to be saved from the consequences of sin. Someday we will meet the Lord in judgment.

> **"For we must all appear before the judgement seat of Christ; that everyone may receive the things done in his body, according to that he hath done, whether it be good or bad."**
>
> **2 Corinthians 5:10**

My experience of being born as a female child, in a community that the culture holds high regard only for a male child, is not wonderful at all. I am the first child of my parents, with two sisters. We are all beautiful, creative and talented, but that's not what parents who believe in a culture that is biased want; they want male children even if they are useless.

My mother married my father as a virgin when she was 18 years of age. She gave birth to three of us, but unfortunately, she couldn't bear a male child, so her life became one of torture, torment, and lamentation every day. Tears became her water to drink. At every slight mistake, she would attract heavy beatings and insults, reminding her of how she could not even bear a male child.

My father's physical abuse of our mother became too violent. We were denied most basic things because we were girls. Our mother tried in her little efforts and raised us, sponsoring us through education from her petty trading. As if that wasn't enough, when our father suddenly died, our mother was accused of killing him to take everything for us. She was openly beaten by my uncles, humiliated, and disgraced. We were thrown out of our father's house and treated as outcasts.

My mother took us to live in another part of the city, away from where our father used to work. A 'Good Samaritan' (female) in my father's workplace helped my mother to get some of the benefits from our father's employers and we started our life of struggle with the small amount she got. She then started a petty trading business, but still life was a struggle to survive daily.

Some days we would pray with our mother and sleep with an empty stomach because her small trading wasn't bringing much profit, and our school fees and medical bills sometimes ate the best part of the capital. However, we all managed to go to school and graduated with good jobs to help take care of our mother.

My problem is, how long will this inhumane culture prevail for? Does culture exist to punish others or does culture exist to give people a sense of belonging with norms and values? Why do people use culture to be wicked to others?

Anonymous

The strength of a strong woman is unbelievable

I married my husband at the age of 13, when I was in secondary school form two. My parents gave me in marriage to my husband as a teenager. I started having children in my teens, before I was 20 years old. I had 3 beautiful girls. That was when my ordeal started. As I could not bear a male child, my husband's mistress got pregnant for him and the scan showed it was a boy. She told my husband and I was sent out of my husband's house with a strong warning never to use his name with my daughters (or prostitutes as he called my daughters). It was a sad moment for me, however, I had to be strong for my girls. So, I picked up the pieces, and started life again as a single mother. Unfortunately, the son that was born to him has health issues.

I went back to my father's house and went back to secondary school. I trained myself and put my girls through school. I went further to enrol in the State University, whilst being an active politician. I was blessed that I got benefit through my politics and occupied a good position within State politics. I have stabilized and secured a future for myself and my girls.

Later on, I graduated from University and continued with political career. My ex-husband made sure he did everything possible to blackmail me. Some of those he spoke with came back to tell me. Some would laugh at his ignorance and ignore him, but he never stopped to go to any extent to destroy me and my daughters and make life miserable for us.

However, God has been our defender, we are **"saved by grace."** By God's grace, I am doing well, and my daughters are doing exceedingly well in their various schools. My advice to all women is be determined and trust in the Lord with all your heart. What the enemy wants to use to destroy you, use to advance yourself and stay strong.

Anonymous

The wounds of this culture curse can be unbearable

We were **"saved by grace."** I am forever grateful to God for His amazing grace upon me and my mother, who have both suffered severely from the evil culture that makes a female child a curse. The afflictions of this evil culture can be unbearable. My mum got married to my dad in Church, and their marriage was blessed with four beautiful girls. However, my dad was not contented with what God had given him and became greedy. He set out from God's way to look for male children that would bear his name when he was dead. That was how our ordeal started. Growing up as a child we experienced so much joy and happiness with our parents, and we thought our dad was very happy and satisfied to have us as his children. But no, he wasn't, because we were only girls and we were not good enough.

In his search for a male child, he got married to a second wife, who bore two boys and two girls for our dad and that was the beginning of our dad's misery in life. The second wife's financial demands from dad were higher than our dad's earnings and when she asked and dad failed to give to her, there was always a fight in the house. She would fight my dad and sometimes our mum would give him the money to give her so that the fight would end.

This behaviour continued until one day dad had a stroke and did not recover from it. As if that wasn't enough, the real trouble started after dad's death – the struggles for dad's properties. Sadly, dad willed most of his properties to me and my sisters because we were very well behaved and excelling at school. We never fought our stepmother nor our half-siblings, although there were often irritations from them, especially the boys. Our mother taught us never to respond to their irritations. Still, that was not good enough for our stepmother, who would always start a fight with our mum, and call her names and accuse her of being jealous of her because she had boys. Our mum would walk away from her without fighting back, but she would not stop until she had reminded her of her inability to bear a male child. Sadly, our uncles were supporting our stepmother in her evil ways.

After my dad's will was read, my uncles insisted that the will must be altered, as we were girls and were not supposed to inherit our fathers' properties since our dad had two boys, and so they should inherit the properties against our father's wish. This resulted in my stepmother going berserk and poisoning my two younger sisters. I was not around that day, otherwise, I would have been dead too. My mother was heartbroken by this wickedness and we moved out of the family house to one of the properties we were given. The threats from our uncles didn't stop, they kept threatening our mum to surrender the properties back to the boys or else all of us would die.

My mum was a woman of prayer, a spiritual fighter; she embraced her faith and taught me to always be prayerful.

One day, one of the vilest uncles who was supporting our stepmother was coming down to meet her to carry out their wickedness. He had an accident on the way and died at the scene. We all went for his burial, as it was the custom to attend funerals of family members. After the burial, I came back with my mum, but my stepmother stayed behind in the village to come back the next day. On her way back she had a terrible accident with her two boys and both of the boys sadly died at the scene. She survived but later died in the hospital. Before she passed, she confessed all her wickedness and asked for our mum's forgiveness, saying that it was the devil's work with the assistance of our uncle that died. He was the one supporting her to do all the evil against my mum. She said she was sorry for the death of our father and my two younger sisters that she had caused. She begged my mum to find it in her heart to forgive her and take her two girls as her own daughters and look after them, as they were innocent.

I narrate this to you fathers who are never satisfied with what God has given you. Be careful; not all that glitters is gold. My dad was a good man, but he was deceived by this culture that puts preference on a boy child over a girl child.

Anonymous

Sad ending for my mum

Where do I start? With tears in my eyes, I narrate the ordeal my mother went through, all for the sake of a culture that prefers a male child over a female child. No matter how well behaved and intelligent the girl child is, you are not good enough, since you cannot bear your father's name when he is dead. What is this thing about a male child? Is it not God that gives children? Does a woman decide the sex of her child in the womb? What crime do women commit when they can't bear a male child? Are girls not children? What sort of culture is this? Why punish women when they can't have male children? Is this culture a curse or a blessing?

I hate discussing this topic because it irritates me so much. Unfortunately, I am a victim of this terrible culture curse. My mum got married to my dad at 16 years of age, had five of us with my dad but could not bear a male child, and so her predicament began. There was much pressure on my dad to take a second wife from family members who were depending on my dad to survive. He yielded to their advice and had a child with a mistress, and he rented an apartment for her and her son. They stayed in a duplex while we were in a flat with our mother.

The flat we were staying in was rented accommodation, my dad did not own the house. Little did my mum know that dad was building a very beautiful modern house and he moved his wife from where they were staying into the new house. My mother protested in vain because all the wider family were supporting dad. My mum became depressed. Dad was spending more time with his son than with us. Daddy was doing well in his job, and all his benefits were invested in the son's name. Dad had an accident and was hospitalised for months and my mum was the one in the hospital with him; unfortunately, we lost him.

When we went for the burial, the custom during a funeral is to introduce the members of the deceased persons family from the wife, the first child to the last. To our great surprise, the family called the second wife first and introduced her with her son and then said the deceased had another wife with five girls. Other family members condemned that and asked that the introduction to be reversed. After the burial, the will was read, and our dad had willed all his properties to his son, including the furniture in our house that we bought before the boy was born.

He stated that his son should allow my mum to have the parlour and bedroom in one of the rented properties, with no furniture, no light, no water, a shared kitchen, shared toilet, and an open yard compound.

We had no choice, and so my mum moved there, however, the humiliation, shame, emotional and mental torture was too much for her to bear. She didn't last long after our father's death and died.

The betrayal from family members I grew up to know as my family is unforgivable, however, my faith tells me to forgive and move on and that is exactly what I have done. My concerns are for how long this culture will keep tormenting women. Who is going to put a stop to this nonsense? The beneficiaries of this culture are very happy, as though they have the power to decide the sex of their children. For how long will the men keep using you women against your fellow women in the name of male children? Do you get benefits from treating fellow women in disrespectful ways? My advice to women who use God's blessing to torment other women is that they should repent, because there is judgement after life here on earth.

Do unto others what you have them do unto you.

Anonymous

I was punished as though I made myself to be barren

When my husband died, I cried and cried, because I knew my world had come to an end. Immediately after the burial, my property was thrown outside, out of my house while the family members mocked me saying that I have no inheritance from the family. They said I am not supposed to stay in the main house where I had lived all my life with my late husband and that I should go to the boys' quarters where I belong. In fact, I have never witnessed or experienced such in my life.

I was in a mess just because I did not have a child.

Name withheld

True life story: A female struggle to go through education above all odds

I got married suddenly at the age of fifteen. I returned from school one day and my mother surreptitiously dragged me into her room. The look in her eyes made me tremble with fear. "My daughter, your father is giving you out this week," she told me bitterly. I could sense from her tone that she was not happy. She'd been very enthusiastic about me going to school. According to her, her childhood friend who sometimes visited us and gave us some beverages and foodstuff, had gone to school, found a very good job, lived in a big house, bought a big car, and married a rich man. Mama believed that she too would have ended up like her friend if her own parents were as enlightened and rich as her friend's parents.

"If my parents were as rich as her parents, I would never have ended up in your father's house," she always lamented sorrowfully.

I felt bad whenever she talked in that manner. The palpable bitterness in her tone made me sick. It seemed that there was a vacuum so large that she wanted me to fill. She often told me that if I could study hard, I would become richer than her friend.

It was for this reason that I studied hard. I remembered when I was leaving primary school in beautiful colours, my teacher had advised my father to make sure I at least completed secondary school. "She is a very brilliant girl and must be encouraged Sir," my teacher had told my father.

"Certainly, I will make sure she goes to secondary school." My father promised but he never did. It was one Aunty who was managing the local health centre in our village, and who was the only nurse in my area, that put me in school. This woman was God-sent; she was known to all in our village. She liked me because at dawn I would sweep the entire clinic before leaving for school. I usually helped them to fetch water from the borehole too.

When my mother told me that afternoon that my father was giving me out, I felt anger surge through my bones. I hadn't expected in my wildest dreams that such a thing would ever happen to me. I was already in SS2 and doing great. If I was allowed to finish, I was sure that my performance would be outstanding.

I ran to my Aunty, the nurse, that evening to tell her what my father was planning to do. She was very furious. "No, it can't happen under my nose! That is not fair. He can't do a thing like that," she screamed in disgust. She went to talk to my father, but he remained adamant about it. He told her bluntly that the decision had already been made. "If her husband desires for her to return to school, he will send her back to school. What use is educating a girl child when her life will be spent outside her father's house?"

So, against my wish and will, I was married to a man who already had two wives. He was forty-one years old, a man twenty-six years older than me. He at that time was already married to two other women who had each given him four children. He was a farmer. I was told that my father's bosom friend was the go-in-between.

Because I was the only 'literate' wife that he married, he promised that he was not going to let me bend my back on the farm with the other wives, but all that ended after I had my first daughter. He pushed me to the farm and became very hostile towards me. It got worse when I became pregnant with my second daughter. According to him, I was a liability. Before my second pregnancy, I got a job as a salesgirl at a fuel station, but he stopped me from working there because according to him, I was going to be exposed and corrupted by some of the young girls working there. No one feels threatened by literacy and civilization more than he does. His inferiority complex and insecurity could consume ten elephants.

One day, seven months into my pregnancy, I was too weak to go to the farm and complained to him. He insisted that I must come along and threatened that if I didn't, I was going to regret ever knowing him. I was already living in regret. In spite of his threats, I refused to go to the farm that day. That was the beginning of my woes. He stopped giving me food and began to treat me like trash. His first wife was the one that would sneak in sometimes to bring me food in my hut. My daughter and I grew pale and sick. One day, I decided to take the matter to the community chief. When my husband was summoned, he told the chief that he was no longer interested in marrying me.

"No, you can't say that now, having already made her pregnant," the chief told him. "You put her in this condition and must fend for her and her child until she is delivered of the baby." So reluctantly, he began to give us food to eat but still detested me. Three months after I had my second child, I gathered my things and left for my home village. I could not bear the harsh treatment anymore. My parents called him, but he said he was not interested in the union again. I later heard that he was getting married to another woman.

Disappointed, my mother challenged my father in my presence for the very first time. "When are you sending me to my own father's house? Can you see how you men destroy the lives of women? Can you see how you treat us as rags? You destroyed me. Now, you have destroyed your first daughter."

Every passing day, as I always did when I was still with my husband, I would cry profusely. One day, after we returned from my father's farm, I met my daughter lying down on the bench shivering. I quickly fetched water and bathed her. I gave her paracetamol and it helped in bringing down the temperature. But at dawn, she got worse. My aunty the nurse had gone to her village for her traditional marriage and her clinic had been shut down since she left. I could only take my daughter to the chemist. My mother had given me four hundred Naira to buy some drugs. "Please take her to the hospital," I was told at the chemist.

I was shocked when the chemist man advised me to take her to the hospital because even though she was ill, she didn't look malnourished. My mother suggested I call the father. He hadn't bothered to come and see his children since we left his house. Not even once did he call to ask about us, never mind sending money for the kids' upkeep.

When I called him, he sent a motorcycle rider to come and pick us up. The motorcyclist took us to a clinic where he and one of his cousins were waiting. The physician that attended to my daughter said that she needed blood. The father said he just returned from the farm and didn't think he had the strength to give his daughter blood! He sent for his nephew who came on a motorcycle. According to him, his nephew was more eligible to give his daughter blood because he was chubby and much younger.

When the nephew was tested and the blood matched, he complained that he had not eaten and would like to eat before he would let anyone take blood from him. The pathetic attitude of these people gave me goose bumps. I watched feebly as he with his cousin and nephew left the clinic for the canteen. "We will be back soon," he told me nonchalantly.

I wished I could donate the blood myself, but the physician had earlier said I could not because I was still breastfeeding my baby, who at that time was eight months old. Tearfully, I held my three-year-old daughter in my arms and began to wait patiently for them. A Fulani man was washing his feet in front of a well at the clinic. When my daughter saw him, she pointed at him weakly and signalled that she was thirsty. I got up and went out to buy her a pack of sachet water. I let her head rest on my shoulder as I carried her to where I bought the water. It was when I returned with her to the clinic that I sensed for the very first time that she was dead. My daughter died like a cockroach while we waited for her father and his relatives to return from the canteen and give her blood. Like a pack of cards, my world came crashing before me. Her father's people returned and took her corpse away for burial.

I thought tragedy was done with me, but I was wrong. Exactly one week after my first daughter died and was buried, my second daughter took ill. Aunty nurse was not back yet. I called the father and he again sent a motorcyclist to come and pick me up. Like my first daughter, my second daughter died in my arms on our way to the clinic. In one week, motherhood slipped miserably from my arms.

When Aunty nurse returned, she advised me to dust off my school bag and go back to school. I began to work with her and because schools were on holiday at that time, she got me two private teachers to coach me at her clinic in the evenings. I was beginning to get my life back together again and hoping to return to school, when my estranged husband came with his people one evening to see my father. They began to beg, saying it had been the devil's work, and they had discovered that his second wife was the one who through spiritual means had turned his heart away from me. I don't know how much they gave to my father because he was grinning from ear to ear and was in total support of me embarking on another journey to slavery.

I was also surprised to see my mother smiling in total submission. It was when she winked at me knowingly that I sensed she had a plan. Upon their departure, my estranged husband gave my mother some money and gave me two five hundred-naira notes. My mother promised him that I was going to return to his house in two days. "We will bring her the day after tomorrow," she said. Another wink at me confirmed totally that my mother was being mischievous. Even my father did not know that she had a plan. It was at night that she took me secretly to Aunty nurse's clinic, where we planned my exit from the village the next day. Surreptitiously, I gathered a bit of my clothing with my books and hid them at Aunty nurse's place. Aunty nurse gave me ten thousand naira and my mother gave me four thousand. It was the money that my estranged husband had given her. "Your father sent you on a journey which produced a bad result and put us all in grief and sorrow. I am sending you now on another journey. Go my daughter and make us proud." As my mother spoke, tears rolled down her cheeks. I promised to make her proud that night.

Very early in the morning the next day, Aunty nurse drove me in her car to the park where I boarded a bus to Abuja, which was where my mother's educated friend and her family were living at that time. My mother had already talked with her on the phone and she had agreed that I should come. I was told that my father threatened fire and brimstone when he heard that I had disappeared. He was told that I was eighteen years old and could decide what to do with my life myself. When my estranged husband came days later to throw tantrums, Aunty nurse gave my mother twenty thousand naira to pay him off. I doubt if he spent as much as that marrying me.

Many years have passed. I am now a resident doctor in Turkey where I graduated with flying colours. But for the opportunity my Aunty the nurse and my Aunty in Abuja, my mum's friend who took me in and sponsored me, my life would have been a total mess. She put all her resources together to ensure that I got the best education. I have turned the story of my family around and proved to all that failure is not a total defeat but a staircase to success. Only last month, I sent some money to the chief of my community for palliatives and medical materials to help fight the COVID-19 pandemic. I am forever grateful to all those who made this second journey of mine a success. I am the first medical doctor from my village, I am a survivor to the glory of God.

Anonymous

The male child syndrome

I have four girls and they are not seen as human beings. But I know that all my tears today will be laughter tomorrow even as my husband has abandoned us and is living with the woman that gave birth to a baby boy for him. I am taking care of the girls alone as if I brought them alone into this wicked world. We are barely surviving, even though their father is wealthy. His second wife does not allow him to help us because she said it is a waste of resources on mere girls who are prostitutes.

She is a woman like me, I leave her to God who is the judge of all. What crime have I and my girls committed?

Name withheld

Women who have male children and mock their women counterparts should be ashamed of themselves. Children are a gift from God, no one gets them by merit. These baby manufacturers as they see themselves are misinformed; it's all about material gain and inheritance. No woman on earth deserves to have children over another. Children are gifts from God, and He gives to anyone regardless, lest you pride yourself in deserving them. These stories are sad; however, similar stories occurred in the Bible as in the case of Sarah and Hagar her slave girl:

> "So, after Abram had lived ten years in the land of Canaan, Sarai, Abram's wife, took Hagar the Egyptian, her slave-girl, and gave her to her husband Abram as a wife. [4] He went into Hagar, and she conceived; and when she saw that she had conceived, she looked with contempt on her mistress. [5] Then Sarai said to Abram, "May the wrong done to me be on you! I gave my slave-girl to your embrace, and when she saw that she had conceived, she looked at me with contempt. May the LORD judge between you and me!
>
> **Genesis 16:3-5**

And also, in the case of Hannah and Peninnah:

> "Because the LORD had closed Hannah's womb, her rival kept provoking her in order to irritate her. This went on year after year. Whenever Hannah went up to the house of the LORD, her rival provoked her till she wept and would not eat. Her husband Elkanah would say to her, "Hannah, why are you weeping? Why don't you eat? Why are you downhearted? Don't I mean more to you than ten sons?"
>
> **1 Samuel 1:6-8**

When you hear stories like this from the victims, it is hard to hold back tears. Many are the afflictions of the righteous, but the Lord God Almighty delivered them from it all. The heart of man is desperately wicked. The issue of childbearing is strictly determined by God. Not a woman or man. We all need to understand this fact to stop putting unnecessary burdens on women.

Imagine it was your mother being treated like that, or your sister or your daughter, how would you feel?

When God blesses a woman with a child, husbands must be grateful regardless of the gender. I understand your preference for a son to bear the family name, however a daughter is precious as well. Include them in your will and make provisions for them to avoid such stories as we have just read from occurring time upon time.

Men, please don't make your wives and daughters suffer when you are gone. Write a will and include them, making provision for your daughters' upkeep, as well as your wife. When a wife dies, her family doesn't come to fight over her inheritance with her husband. Make the burden lighter.

My humble counsel to female children and womenfolk

I was a victim. Though my father died without any property, just the little farm that was collected from us, I did not allow the wrong done to me to hold me back. I asked God to forgive me where I was wrong and grant me the forgiving spirit to forgive those who hurt me, and I moved on.

Understanding the benefit of forgiveness really helps to get over your past hurt. Forgiveness heals you, the forgiver, more than the forgiven. So, I made up my mind to forgive those who intentionally hurt me. At that point, I received my own forgiveness from God for the wrong things I had done knowingly or unknowingly. By doing this, I freed myself to move on.

Women do not allow any encumbrance to limit you from God's blessing; forgive as to be forgiven. This is my sincere advice to all who have been hurt in any way. Remember we are all human beings and it is only human to react when we are hurt, however, to err is human but to forgive is divine. I empathise with all of you that have been maltreated for being a girl. Do not allow any encumbrance to limit you.

When someone hurts us, our natural response is to either hurt them back or hope they will suffer for what they've done. But as children of God who have been forgiven and saved, we know this is the wrong response.

Forgiving someone doesn't come naturally or easily; it requires supernatural grace on our part. We get that through prayer. Jesus said:

"When you stand praying if you hold anything against anyone, forgive them, so that your Father in heaven may forgive you your sins."

Matthew 6:15

When we remember how God has shown grace toward us, we realise that we need to show that same grace to those who have hurt us. Sometimes we can feel that we have a right to hold on to unforgiveness, or that if we forgive people, we're letting them get away with what they did to us. But actually, if we don't forgive people, we're keeping ourselves tied to the hurt and the person who caused it. Bitterness and unforgiveness actually destroy us more in the long run. The people who have hurt us will be judged by God. He calls us to forgive people, just as He has forgiven us.

If there's a gift that I know that young girls have, it is the strength of character and the ability to look the world in the face and tell it that it was wrong about you and then go become all that you are meant to. This gift is latent and lying dormant in many. Sometimes, it takes some tribulation to unlock it, much like the sweet coconut water is only released when the coconut is drilled or crushed.

The world would peddle stereotypes meant to stifle you: don't buy it. Society would bestow barriers that can clip your wings: burst them. And some cultures would try to harness you - break the harness. There are no walls, no bars, no ceilings, no boxes that can limit you.

Christ is telling you today that you can do all things because He has strengthened you.

> **"I can do all things through him who strengthens me".**
>
> **Philippians 4:13**

3

TRIALS OF FEMALE INFERTILITY

"And when Rachel saw that she bore Jacob no children, Rachel envied her sister; and said unto Jacob, give me children, or else I die. And Jacob's anger was kindled against Rachel: and he said, Am I in God's stead, who hath withheld from thee the fruit of the womb? And she said, Behold, my maid Bilhah, go in unto her; and she shall bear upon my knees, that I may also have children by her".

Genesis 30: 1-3.

Society's Problems and the Girl Child

There is a general belief in many societies across Nigeria, especially among the **Tiv people**, that the wife is accountable each time a female is born. Yet the husband takes the praise upon the birth of a male child. This notion has made many men divorce their wives for the failure to produce a male child. Even, in the absence of an outright divorce, some lenient husbands go ahead to marry a second wife and when the newly married wife eventually bears a son, all attention is shifted to her and most times, with the first wife not being able to bear the maltreatment further, she and her daughters are compelled to move out of the house. This brings to the fore one of the many ills of male child preference in **Tivland**, which is the fact that it has led many married men into committing **an offence against the state, which is bigamy (the offence of marrying someone while already married to another person).**

Scientifically, this assumption that women are exclusively responsible for the gender of a child is misleading, as it has been established by science (genetics) that during the mating, it is only when the male releases the Y-chromosomes to fuse with the X-chromosomes released by the female that a male foetus is formed. So, the man is even more responsible for the gender of a child.

Across many societies in Nigeria, being a woman exposes one to untold vulnerabilities and disadvantages. This patriarchal tradition is an age-long one. Despite advances in science and technology, the problem of inequality and inequity is not one that can be eradicated by fact, or that one acquires immunity from via a vaccine. You come across girls and women despising the privilege of being female, wishing they were born males to improve their lot in life. Gender roles have been assigned and women bear a considerable burden in society. For some people, a girl child is unwanted or at best objectified. Many girls and women have come to accept their place in the pecking order of gender. In such situations, girls are subliminally blamed for being born a female (when it was a male child that was desired), and when she comes of age (if she is allowed to), she is shamed for being single, almost as though she could only be valued on the altar of matrimony. If she gets married, she is shamed for infertility (even if it's not her fault), then if she conceives, she is shamed for having girls (despite the science). If she has sons and daughters who do not turn out right, she is shamed for their poor upbringing and blamed for the moral decline in society. Never has society expected so much to whom it has given so little! And so many girls go around not knowing who they are, lost in a cold world.

The issue of male child preference to the detriment of the girl child often grows with the girl child into womanhood. What today's girl learns from the upbringing ultimately affects tomorrow's woman and tomorrow's mother. How can this culture curse be broken? This culture is destroying a lot of women's lives. The pressure of it can be unbearable at times.

The desperation of a tortured, humiliated and rejected woman

A desperate woman who is in dire need of having a child at all costs to maintain her marriage is willing to take risks in order to change her predicament, as we read in the scriptural quote in Genesis, about Rachel's rash reaction and in a hasty decision that led her giving her concubine to the husband to bear children for her to maintain her position in her marriage.

O dear husband, you need to understand what your wife is already going through and stop making her feel frustrated, rejected, and having to go through so much torture just because she loves you and could risk her life to prove her commitment to you. Why can't you treat your wives with mercy, love, and kindness?

Desperation is a negative emotion from someone who is seriously in trouble. Desperate people can be overwhelmed with their problems, not knowing what to do, and if possible, finding others to help them, just like Rachel did by giving her husband her maidservant to bear children for her.

Desperation is a strong feeling of sadness, fear, and loss of hope. Given the opportunity, no woman would ordinarily want to be a barren woman, nor bear only daughters. So, for a woman to have at least female children should be a thing of joy to both husband and wife, not a curse. God Himself has acknowledged the importance of a female child in the Bible and asked Moses to make the girl child relevant and recognised legally.

> "The daughters of Zelophehad son of Hepher, the son of Gilead, the son of Makir, the son of Manasseh, belonged to the clans of Manasseh, son of Joseph. The names of the daughters were Mahlah, Noah, Hoglah, Milkah, and Tirzah. They came forward [2] and stood before Moses, Eleazar the priest, the leaders, and the whole assembly at the entrance to the tent of meeting and said, [3] "Our father died in the wilderness. He was not among Korah's followers, who banded together against the LORD, but he died for his own sin and left no sons. [4] Why should our father's name disappear from his clan because he had no son? Give us property among our father's relatives". So, Moses brought their case before the LORD, and the LORD said to him, "What Zelophehad's daughters are saying is right. You must certainly give them property as an inheritance among their father's relatives and give their father's inheritance to them. "Say to the Israelites, 'If a man

dies and leaves no son, give his inheritance to his daughter. If he has no daughter, give his inheritance to his brothers. If he has no brothers, give his inheritance to his father's brothers. If his father had no brothers, give his inheritance to the nearest relative in his clan, that he may possess it. This is to have the force of law for the Israelites, as the LORD commanded Moses."

Numbers 27:1-11

The definition of culture includes our religious beliefs; why then do we select some parts of the Scriptures that favour us and neglect other parts as deemed less important?

When you take time to speak with a woman going through this emotional torture, you can't hold back tears, it is really heart-breaking to hear these stories from the victims themselves. Most couples get married as husband and wife because of the true love that binds them together and agreed to marry each other without the condition that the wife must have male children. Children are a blessing from the union; a good marriage must not be maintained because it is blessed with children. Why allow the enemy to come into the beautiful love story you both created for yourselves? Are children the reason why you both got married in the first place? We call ourselves devoted Christians, where is Christ in us in all this?

Interestingly, on our beautiful wedding days, the issue of children is never included in the vows couples take before joining together as husband and wife. They say all sorts of sweet promises on that day, but the sweet vows are deleted as soon as a child is not forthcoming: why? It's a shame that even some African men who are resident in Western countries have this mentality as well.

On my Registry marriage day (**26th July 2003**), my husband asked that this song by Celine Dion was played and he dedicated the song to our love story. He even wrote the words down as a gift for me and made it his ringtone on his phone when I called him. It rang with the song to constantly remind him of our love. It was the ringtone on my phone when he called me as well. I believed every word of the song coming from his heart. I have kept this precious gift in my treasured box. So, just imagine that he changes due to my inability to have children or to have male children for him; is that not a heart-breaking deception? Fortunately, I have the best husband in the whole wide world, and the issues of children were never an issue to him at all. He was the strong one when I started to worry too much. He was more concerned about my happiness. Below is what he wrote before writing out the song for me as a reminder of our love story.

"Hi Sweetheart,
You are the best wife in the whole wide world! (BWITWWW)

This is the song I played on our wedding day and I am dedicating it for us as a reminder of our love and commitment to each other, it is your ringtone on my mobile as well. Sounds as if it was composed of our lives together in mind".

BECAUSE YOU LOVED ME
CELINE DION

For all those times you stood by me
For all the truth that you made me see
For all the joy you brought to my life
For all the wrong that you made right
For every dream, you made come true
For all the love I found in you

I'll be forever thankful baby
You're the one who held me up
Never let me fall
You're the one who saw me through... through
it all

You were my strength when I was weak
You were my voice when I couldn't speak
You were my eyes when I couldn't see
You saw the best there was in me
Lifted me up when I couldn't reach
You gave me faith 'coz you believed
I'm everything I am
Because you loved me

You gave me wings and made me fly
You touched my hand I could touch the sky
I lost my faith, you gave it back to me
You said no star was out of reach
You stood by me and I stood tall
I had your love I had it all
I'm grateful for each day you gave me
Maybe I don't know that much
But I know this much is true
I was blessed because I was loved by you

You were my strength when I was weak ....

You were always there for me
The tender wind that carried me
A light in the dark shining your love into my life
You've been my inspiration
Through the lies you were the truth
My world is a better place because of you

You were my strength when I was weak ....

GOD BLESS
Yours truly,
Best husband in the whole world (BHITWW).

****

The vows we made to our spouses during
wedding ceremonies are very powerful, and
when the love wine is running out, all we need
to do is to go back and reflect on those vows and
meditate on them and ask the Holy Spirit to
strengthen us and refill the love wine. I am very
fortunate to have a God-fearing man as a
husband; he is so different, and the issue of not
having children was not much of a problem to
him; he was always the stronger person,
encouraging me to keep the switch of faith
turned on while we waited for God's time.

Though the pressure was a lot on him back home in Nigeria, he used to say God is the only person who gives children so don't think too much about it. People will always talk, however, what matters is united we stand, divided we fall. God made it possible at His appointed time. Medically I had no problem with infertility though I had fibroids, but the doctors told us it was nothing that would prevent me from conceiving. I had an operation and it was removed. I had three miscarriages before we had our first beautiful daughter and after that, I had two further miscarriages. After the last miscarriage the fibroid came back again, and this time I almost died during the operation. The doctors told us at this point that, I had less than 5% chance of ever becoming pregnant again. Scary isn't it? However, our most powerful God suddenly showed up and refilled our love wine again. I became pregnant supernaturally with my little boy.

I love these words in the song Jesus (You are able) by Ada Ehi:

> *Creator of the universe, what can't you do, what can't you do... Jesus?*

*Your name is above every other name, what
can't you change, what can't you change
...Jesus?*

*You are able Great and mighty God, you
are able... Jesus*

*There's nothing, nothing you cannot do,
nothing you cannot change, nothing you
cannot turn around...You are able Great
and mighty God, I put my trust in you, you
are able Jesus.*

This song touches my heart and whenever I am singing the song, I soak myself in the words so that I forget my worries knowing He is able. In truth, He is able. He changed the reports of the doctors concerning me and I became pregnant. Isn't our God able and awesome? **During the pregnancy, the enemy showed up and the pregnancy went into pre-eclampsia and I had to go through a caesarean section to remove the baby at six months, six days. My condition became very difficult, I had a 40% and the baby had a 60% chance of surviving after the section. My faith in God was too strong to start doubting Him at this point. I trusted Him with all my heart and leaned not on my own feelings** nor understanding. He showed forth for me and we both survived to the glory of God. It was a miracle that the doctors could not explain.

> "Trust in the LORD with all thine heart and lean not unto thine own understanding. In all thy ways acknowledge him, and he shall direct thy paths."
>
> Proverb 3:5-6

These things are easier said than done, especially when you are in that situation. It seems as though your whole world has come to an end, especially if you don't have a husband who puts your feelings first. It becomes a challenge; however, pulling through barrenness together moves God to show forth.

I had a friend who was thrown out of her husband's house because of infertility after eight years of marriage without a child, but as soon as she left to start her life all over again, she became pregnant with another man. This man proposed and married her; they have four children now. Her ex-husband was influenced by his family to send her away. He allowed them to manipulate him, and he has remained in regret each time I speak with him. He allowed the influence of others to rob him of his first love. Husbands be patient with your wives; God is exceedingly able to bless your marriages, if only you can trust Him with your heart desires to perfect them.

The anguish women go through when they are suffering infertility alone is enough. Adding to their pains by rejection, emotional abuse, physical abuse, name-calling, and throwing them out of your lives is never the solution. I have a close relative who has been married to his wife for more than twenty years now without a child; however, their love blossoms every time I see them or speak with them. They appreciate each other so much; they have not allowed the family pressure or cultural influence to affect their feelings for each other at all. This is how it should be.

Interestingly, some of those children these men insist on having by marrying other wives or engaging their girlfriends to bear for them are in most cases not even their biological children. Ask such a man to go and do DNA testing with such children; you will hear so many senseless excuses such as that the culture of Tiv man does not allow them to carry out DNA testing on their children to avoid stigma. Really? But the culture of this same Tiv man allows him to send his wife away because of infertility? What a twisted culture, that is only made to favour the men.

Many married women sleep around with other men apart from their husbands in search of a male. child. Most of these women end up carrying dirty secrets all their lives knowing they have been unfaithful. Why would a woman defile her marriage out of desperation for a male child? That is allowing the culture made by men to destroy your integrity, dignity, and respect. Many homes are broken because of infidelity. Why allow the culture and your desperation to maintain a marriage that is already spiritually broken the day you cheated on your husband? Why can't you trust God and wait for His timing? If He doesn't give you a child, then trust His plan for your life more than trusting in mortal men that can disappoint you anytime.

> **"It is better to take refuge in the LORD than to put confidence in mortals."**
> **Psalm 118:8.**

I pray for the day this culture will be redressed and DNA added to the co-values of the so-called culture. Many homes in Tivland will break up. There will be many untimely deaths because most male children will discover they are not the biological children of their fathers. Infidelity is another evil act practiced in the name of protecting a biased culture. Would you rather a stranger takes over your property than your own biological female children? Fathers, think of the damage and consequences you are doing to your daughters. I have known a family of five girls who are all lawyers, very successful, and another family of three girls: one is a medical doctor, another a lawyer, and the last one an architect, all very successful in their careers. It is not a guarantee for boys to be more successful than girls. Both just need opportunity and support from their parents.

****

I spoke to a rejected woman and here is her real-life story:

My husband suffered infertility and died a broken man

My husband had diabetes and did not treat it well before we got married, so it resulted in complications which included affecting his fertility. I realised this problem just after we got married. I told him not to worry, that we were in it together. I promised him my commitment to support him. I advised him to consult a medical professional which he did, but unfortunately, it was a little too late to correct the damage, as he had left it for too long. His family didn't know much about his problem and kept pressuring him to marry another wife to bear his children accusing me of being barren. The family pressure made his condition worse and he developed high blood pressure, had a stroke, and sadly died.

I was blamed for his death without a child to bear his name and hated by the family, through no fault of my own. However, I didn't try to explain to them that it wasn't my fault, because even if I had told them the truth at this time, they would not have believed me, nor would they have accepted the medical reports I had about him. I was treated very badly by my in-laws and thrown out of my husband's house; the house I had helped him build with my own money. I was called names and humiliated publicly. My husband was already dead, he couldn't wake from the grave to defend my innocence. I took all the humiliation and physical abuse for loving my late husband and protecting his image among his kinsmen, so that no one would know he was impotent. Such is life. I left without anything. After two years of mourning my husband, I picked up the pieces and started building my life all over again. I married again and I have four children of my own with my new husband.

Anonymous

4

IS THIS CULTURE A BLESSING OR CURSE?

"How shall I curse, whom God hath not cursed? Or how shall I defy, whom the Lord hath not defied?"

Numbers 23:8.

> *"Nobody hides pains better than a mother who's trying to remain strong for her kids."*

Is this culture a blessing or a curse? Even if it is, who can curse whom God hath not cursed? Nevertheless, should we all fold our arms and accept this African tradition that has a patriarchal structure characterised by gender inequality between males and females? Or is it time women spoke out about the difficulties of life and the fate of girls trying to succeed amidst this patriarchal structure?

Male gender preference over female is a dominant feature of Tiv culture. It is strongly perceived among Tiv men and is significantly influenced by socio-demographic factors. Male gender preference may be the reason why some Tiv men marry so many wives and still some keep concubines to bear children for them. The culture of Tiv is very gender sensitive and patriarchal. When a child is born, especially the first-born child, and is a male child, the joy of the father is demonstrated openly. The father is happy because he has a man who will take his place after his death and continue his family lineage. There is joy for the mother because this birth will properly entrench her in her husband's heart.

Having a son means that nothing can uproot her from the family. A son further means having a voice to defend you in the family. However, if the child is a girl, some husbands and wives receive it with mixed feelings. And if the female child is the third, fourth, fifth or sixth female born into the family without a male child, then that is enough for sorrow. For the man, it brings sorrow because his hope of having a male child to continue his lineage is becoming slimmer, and the females will soon be married off to other men.

Having female children is like "tending other people's vineyard while yours is unkept". For this reason, the man starts to consider marrying a second wife or looking outside to have children outside of his marriage, especially if family members have started putting pressure on the man. He either marries another wife or gets a mistress to bear him a male child. Some men will have illegitimate children and keep them away from their wives until after their death, then the male child will resurface and be introduced to the family. Some men will even will all their property to the unknown child and disinherit their daughters for being females. If the legitimate wife is unlucky, she is thrown out of the house by family members with her daughters without any property of her late husband.

This culture is evil and destructive. A male child is seen as being very important by both parents, who place such relevance on a male child over their female children. Very early in their lives, the male children are made to see themselves as superior to the female, which they are not. Based on my interaction with some of the mostly female victims of this culture, it can be deduced that Western education has not had any effect on the Tiv society's preference for the male child. I know of many educated Tiv sons who out of desperation for a male child, married second wives to have children, and some keep mistresses to bear children for them. The desperation at times is from both men and women.

Some women, for fear of being thrown out of their husband's houses or losing their marriage, go to extremes looking for children through ungodly ways. This desperation is because of societal pressure to preserve one's lineage. Anxiety is a displeasing feeling of fear and concern, and if not controlled can lead to depression. It can affect some women's chances of becoming pregnant. The amount of pressure this culture puts on women is too much. However, I totally disagree with women going outside God's will to look for children to maintain their marriages in ungodly ways. Some sleep around with other men in the hope of getting a male child.

Hannah wanted a male child desperately; she went to God who is the giver of children and she got Samuel. She didn't go to gods or run after other men. She sought the counsel of the Lord through fervent prayers.

"Not so, my Lord," Hannah replied, "I am a woman who is deeply troubled. I have not been drinking wine or beer; I was pouring out my soul to the LORD. [16] Do not take your servant for a wicked woman; I have been praying here out of my great anguish and grief." Eli answered, "Go in peace, and may the God of Israel grant you what you have asked of him." She said, "May your servant find favour in your eyes." Then she went her way and ate something, and her face was no longer downcast. Early the next morning they arose and worshipped before the LORD and then went back to their home at Ramah. Elkanah made love to his wife Hannah, and the LORD remembered her. [20] So in the course of time Hannah became

pregnant and gave birth to a son. She named him Samuel, saying, because I asked the LORD for him."

1 Samuel 1:15-20

Women, do not allow the desperation of having male children for your husbands to push you away from seeking children from God, who is the source and giver of the fruit of the womb. Seek first the kingdom of God and all other things shall be added unto you. The Bible said all, and not some, other things. When you are being provoked to be irritated, turn your provocation to God who cares for you. Do not allow the pressures of life to become too much that you go seeking help from evil gods. Take your problems to Almighty God in prayers. He is able to supply all your needs according to His riches in glory.

There are a lot of **"Peninnahs"** out there, and they will provoke, irritate you, and remind you of your inability to bear a male child. You should ignore them and focus on God, trusting Him to take away your reproach. I suffered infertility as well and received provocations from family members, however, the most important person in my life was very supportive, and so we pulled through it with happiness. We appreciate God for the lives of our children Doobee Deborah and Samuel Sefa Adura.

Culturally, a woman is not only married to her husband, but also to his relations to the extent that she accords them the same respect that she gives to her husband. When her husband is not around or has died, she has to contact her husband's male relatives for important decisions like giving her daughter out in marriage. Some of the in-laws are unnecessarily hard to please. Often, some relatives of the husband rile the wife and most families see no wrong in that, feeling that no woman is good enough to be welcomed into the family.

It is also important to note that women virtually have no reproductive rights in rural settings. Men ask the women to lie with them, without giving any thoughts as to whether the woman is tired or ill. It is the men's right to have their way with women whenever they feel like it. The woman has no right to say no. Likewise, men determine the number of children to have regardless of the health condition of the wife. They can marry as many wives as they desire, although this is an offence against the state.

Most of them can't even look after these women and their children, and therefore it is the responsibility of the women to provide for their children. Whenever the men go out and come back home, no matter how late it is, they expect to be served food, and failure to meet these demands leads to physical abuse.

Some husbands bring their mistress into their matrimonial homes and defile their matrimonial bed. The wife mustn't complain. The list goes on and on. Many are the afflictions and burdens women bear for the sake of marriage. Cultural practices have made it so hard for women to air their views. They are forced to always say yes to things without uttering any words of complaint. It is the belief system of patriarchy that actually makes females subordinate to males, and not necessarily because they do not have the moral capacity to fully function as the males do.

Tiv women married in urban areas are not exempted from this: it is virtually the same in both settings. "It is a male's world"; that's how the world sees it. Some of those educated women living with their husbands in the big cities are not immune to the culture curse.

When a woman demonstrates her rights as a woman, her husband and his family tag her to be a bad wife who has her husband under a spell. **Is this culture a blessing or a curse?**

Shall we all fold our arms and carry on suffering under this culture and pretend all is well?

Or is it high time we spoke out and cried for help for our daughters? A closed mouth is a closed destiny; women, speak up. We desire better treatment, respect and love. Enough is enough.

5

BELIEVE IN YOURSELF

"Charm is deceptive, and beauty is fleeting; but a woman who fears the Lord is to be praised."

Proverbs 31:3

"For you created my inmost being; you knit me together in my mother's womb. I praise you because I am fearfully and wonderfully made; your works are wonderful; I know that full well."

Psalm 139:13-14.

153

Patriarchal tradition, women's vulnerabilities and disadvantages

Many women have great hidden talents; however, a society dominated by males has suppressed them so much that their gifts remain hidden and untapped. It took me a long time to realise that I could achieve what I have achieved in my early fifties, because the social pressure on me was so much that I wouldn't have been able to bear it, if God was not on my side. Always appreciate the fact that

> **"Besides God, there is no glory above coming from humble beginnings, from sleeping under a porous grass-thatched mud hut to rising above and beyond tabernacles of greatness."**
>
> (Thabo Katlholo)

I know many women with various talents and gifts. All it takes is for them to develop the ability to look the world in the face and tell it that it was wrong to underestimate them. There are many great women with special talents or abilities lying dormant, and it takes the grace of God to prove their capabilities to the world in His time.

"You can do all things through Him who strengthens you."

Philippians 4:13

My advice to all women is that, remember that at every turn in life, hindrances present themselves and attempt to limit your happiness, talents, and your ability to succeed in the male-dominated society. These hindrances may be painful, cruel, unjust, and can limit you if you let them. Allowing yourselves to be confined by the prison walls of your fears, your "if-only", your past mess-ups, will stop you from blooming and becoming all that the Lord wants for you. Every person regardless of gender has struggled in one form or the other, even the Saints and Prophets.

Be determined and put on the armour of God and fight a good fight for your right.

"Finally, be strong in the Lord and in his mighty power. Put on the full Armour of God, so that you can take your stand against the devil's schemes. For our struggle is not against flesh and blood, but against the rulers, against the authorities, against the powers of this dark world and against the spiritual forces of evil in the heavenly realms. Therefore, put on the full Armour of God, so that when the day of evil comes, you may be able to stand your ground, and after you have done everything, to stand. Stand firm then, with the belt of truth buckled around your waist, with the breastplate of righteousness in place, and with your feet fitted with the readiness that comes from the gospel of peace. In addition to all this, take up the shield of faith, with which you can extinguish all the flaming arrows of the evil one. Take the helmet of salvation and the sword of the Spirit, which is the word of God. And pray in the Spirit on all occasions with all kinds of prayers and requests. With this in mind, be alert and always keep on praying for all the Lord's people. Pray also for me, that whenever I speak, words may be given me so that I will fearlessly make known the mystery of the gospel."

Ephesians 6:0-19.

You have what it takes to succeed. Remove fear from your mind and use any opportunity you have to advance yourselves. Be the **Proverbs 31 woman** in your generation.

Remember,

> **"Many are the afflictions of the righteous, but the Lord delivers them from all."**
>
> **Psalm 34:19**

For one woman, it may be the limit or barriers that the culture or family has created for them. But you don't have to stave off these hindrances alone; in fact, you cannot do it on your own. The Lord Himself will empower you. Human inabilities mean nothing to God, for He delights to manifest Himself in our weaknesses. God's words are yes and amen. Our weakness is not a limitation but a sign of courage. His grace is made available for us.

> **"But he said to me, my grace is sufficient for you, for power is made perfect in weakness. So, I will boast all the more gladly of my weaknesses, so**

that the power of Christ may dwell in
me."

2 Corinthians 12:9.

When you push beyond your limits and allow
God to take over your battles, then it becomes
evident that the hand of the Lord alone has
done it. Cast your cares upon Him; He is faithful
and just. You too can invite Jesus to deal with
the hindrances in your life. Our Lord is not
rude, He is so gentle that He awaits your
invitation and would only come in if you open
the door. By inviting God to work with your
burdens, you can access the Grace that He has
lavished on you so freely. You need to see
yourself as God sees you, not as the world does,
and discover your identity in Christ. Women of
faith, you are empowered by the Spirit of Christ
in you, to be determined and succeed despite the
odds against you. **Go to school and upgrade
yourselves, which is what I did in my late
forties.** It's never too late. Once there is life and
will-power, there is hope. God uses imperfect
things to make perfect things. He uses
unqualified persons to do qualifying things. He
uses your brokenness and vulnerability to make
you strong in the Lord.

Though the foundation of my elementary education was not solid, that did not determine my achievements. I did not have a good elementary academic knowledge as I went to a village primary school where I achieved minimal skills. I only started learning to read in secondary school, and my performance was very poor in all the subjects.

After secondary school, I didn't do well in my first attempt at GCE O' Level, so I went back and repeated two classes, starting all over again from Form 4, and that was when I began to understand most educational concepts and started applying them. This time I did the best I could in GCE O' Level and proceeded to College of Education and did well again.

I wanted to proceed to the university but was constrained by circumstance. I waited for a long time until an opportunity of relocating to the United Kingdom presented itself through my aunt and her husband. Whilst I was in the UK, I met a young, promising gentleman, named Dr Peter Adura, who would later become my husband. Peter Adura was already a practising medical doctor in the UK at the time we met. We became friends and as God would have it, we got married. I was very honest with him, told him all about my past life and my ambition to further my education.

Being a very educated man with a vision to help others achieve their dreams, he encouraged me, and I got enrolled in the Itchen college in Southampton for an Access course to Higher education. I completed the course and acquired the necessary skills needed to enrol in any university in the UK. I applied through UCAS and got offers from 4 Universities in the UK to study Law.

I chose the University of Buckingham, because it was much closer to where we were living at the time and allowed me to drive to university and come home to look after my young children. It wasn't easy at all; I had to bring my mother from Nigeria to babysit for me. God bless her and her enormous support.

I started my undergraduate studies at the age of 47. I graduated with good grades and enrolled immediately for my Master of Law which I also completed with good grades and an award. I then proceeded to the Nigerian Law school, and after the completion of the one year and three months course, I was called to the Nigerian Bar Association as a Barrister and Solicitor of the Supreme Court of Nigeria. I was so determined that whilst in Nigeria I enrolled for two professional courses. One was to become a Chartered Mediator and Conciliator and the other was to become a Chartered Secretary and Administrator. I aced both and got qualified as a fellow of the two Prestigious Chartered Institutes.

Remember this quote:

"Don't underestimate Small Humble Beginnings, because sometimes they can turn out to be the Greatest Success Stories."

(Jeanette Coron)

I have narrated my educational feats to encourage other women who think it's too late for them to go back to school and upgrade themselves. It is never too late. All that matters is one's mindset. **Believe in yourself**! Commit yourself to make a new start, by prayer, and supplication; make your request known to God and He shall direct your path. He did it for me. He will do it for you. Just believe in yourself not what the society has put you through. Refuse to give up. No human being is dull, you just need determination and perseverance.

I have written this, my first book, to fulfil the desires of my golden age. Stir up that spirit of **"I can't do it"** in you; write that book you always wanted; be determined to blaze that trail, to fight that ailment, to break that addiction, to win that award. Now I look back over drinks and celebrate the wonders of God upon my life with family and friends, as I reflect on my story. People who have seen my struggles through these phases say that I am a strong woman. The truth is that, what people call the strength of character, that grit, is the grace of God. And the Lord tells us that His Grace is sufficient enough for us. God's grace is manifest in your life as well.

> **"Every big castle was once started with a single block; despise no small beginnings. A little step taken every day builds up the hope of greater accomplishments. Do something every day!"**
>
> **(Israelmore Ayivor)**

The pains women go through to survive and make a career above all odds, and their dogged determination to pursue a career as a woman in a male-dominated culture is amazing.

Society may have written you off, but what do you feel about yourself? Are you a loser? Can you dig your heels in and prove your worth to the society that rejected and made you a laughingstock? Are you more than determined above all things to achieve your dream?

If I can do it at a very mature age, then you don't have any excuse, get on with it. God's got your back.

6

SUCCESS IS ACHIEVED THROUGH DETERMINATION AND PERSEVERANCE

"If you're trying to achieve something spectacular, there will be roadblocks. I've had them, everybody has them. But obstacles don't have to stop you. If you run into a wall, don't turn around and give up. Figure out how to climb it, go through it, or work around it."

(Michael Jordan)

"A great door for effective work has opened to me, and there are many who oppose me."
1 Corinthians 16:9.

Nothing good comes easy, neither does any success become truly great until it overcomes something that looks insurmountable. Great doors of opportunity always come with great challenges, and each challenge calls for greater faith and tenacity. Think about it: if outstanding success came easily, everyone would have it. And if everyone had it, it wouldn't be an outstanding success. This is why you need determination and perseverance to achieve your dreams. I shared my journey of success in the previous chapter, and that started with a single step. When the going gets tough and it seems that your goal cannot be reached, don't adjust the goal, adjust your action steps.

Thinking of success through determination and perseverance, how does a caterpillar become a butterfly? By overcoming the cocoon. The cocoon is so essential to the process that the caterpillar actually creates it. Wouldn't it be easier just to stay in the warmth and comfort of the cocoon? On days when the caterpillar struggles to get out of it, he probably thinks so! But deep down, he knows the price of freedom. Success and breakthrough require struggle, courage and determination. There is no other way! Why did Jesus send His disciples into a life-threatening storm? To teach them to trust Him in all of life's situations. Soon He'd be leaving them, and He was using every experience to prepare them for their future. So, what are you struggling to overcome right now? Is it fear of failure? Or fear of other factors? You can't achieve success if you don't dare to overcome your biggest fears.

Instead of complaining, being discouraged, throwing pity parties for yourself, and asking God to take it away, see it for what it is: preparing you to achieve. Use your encumbrances as steppingstones to break forth. Remember, your level of preparation indicates the level of blessing that awaits you on the other side of it. I had a very difficult and challenging childhood. It was tough. However, I have broken the barrier and set the record straight. No limitation put on me could stop me and my sisters. We are victorious.

Dear virtuous women, it is not going to be easy, but remember, if God is opening doors of opportunity for you, be prepared for challenges because you can't have one without the other. If you come across any successful women, they have a painful story behind their success in a male-dominated society. There are some women who have achieved their success on a platter of gold, while there are some that when they narrate their success story, your heart will melt with emotions. Be encouraged, you are not alone. I am speaking directly to women reading this book. Smile, Jesus loves you.

I love this quote by Israel Ayivor from his book "Become a better you."

> "Don't just exist; do something meaningful with your life. Discover a problem and fix it. Don't just fit in; make it a point to brighten your corner. Decide to resolve your challenges. Don't just manage; go the extra mile and win your race. Never give up the fight. You will win. Don't just be able; always make sure you are available. Be present to make a change. Don't just be alive; once you have arrived, find the reason why

and make that reason accomplished. Don't just wish; be passionate about what you wish to see happen. Rise up and make it happen. Don't just create; create to change; change to improve; improve to increase. Aspire to inspire. Don't just be making a living; make a life and leave an indelible footstep wherever you step. I want to meet you and many others on the top. Don't be left out!"

Most of the real-life stories narrated in this book were achieved through determination, perseverance, and faith in God. Never underestimate the power of a praying woman. Successful women are not lazy women, they are the bedrock of the family. They have the spirit of **"I can do it"** in them. They do not say no to their dreams, no matter how long it takes. Every woman has that strength of character in them. With tears in their eyes, they can smile and say it is well, God is in control.

I want to encourage every woman to develop that spirit of never giving up on themselves. Push your limit and refuse to be defined by men. Rise to the challenge and tackle all your adversaries head-on. God has our backs. Blessed women of faith, keep the switch of your faith turned on at all times.

7

TRIBUTES TO THE AUTHOR FROM FRIENDS/FAMILY

"Seest thou a man diligent in his business? He shall stand before kings; he shall not stand before mean men"

Proverb 22:29

What is a tribute?

An act, statement, or gift that is intended to show gratitude, respect, or admiration. In other words, a tribute is a sign of respect or admiration, an award to honour a person's accomplishments.

We're most familiar with the use of the word **tribute as meaning to honour someone with words or an award.** You can hear a tribute if you attend a program of entertainment, an award-giving ceremony or a funeral. Tribute, therefore, is something you do or say or make to show your admiration and respect for someone. To write a tribute for someone is to show clearly how good, strong, or effective someone is, or admire their accomplishment in life.

Here we have a set of tributes from friends, family, and well-wishers of the author to show the strength, determination and courage of the author as she pulled through life to achieve her academic feat. From helplessness to greatness.

Tribute by Dr Peter Terfa Adura (Author's husband)

"Many women have done admirable things, but you surpass them all."
                                      Proverbs 31:29 NJB

As you read through my wife's story, you will notice a thread running through it. It is this characteristic of someone who refuses to accept things as they are. Someone with a vision. A vision that things ought to be better, and how they can be better. Armed with that vision from her earliest years, Lois has refused to be a victim of her circumstances. She is a true illustration of the saying: "***Cream always rises to the top.***" Or, maybe, the African version is more apt here: **"*You cannot keep a calabash under water.*"**

I invite you to read all of **Proverbs 31**. You will appreciate even better the context of the above quote. This book of scripture describes her more eloquently, more aptly than I ever could. It is a better tribute than any human could ever have crafted for the virtuous wife that Lois has proved to be. I love you my best wife just the way you are.

Tribute to an elder sister par excellence, my role model and my super woman with dimensional personality

My name is Joyce Ngufan Asuku, the immediate younger sister to Barrister Mrs Lois Hembadoon Adura. I'm always in a tight corner when it's come to me to say something or describe my elder sister; she is a dimensional personality that sometimes is difficult to predict. She is full of surprises. She has many qualities. I can sum it up by say saying this woman is like a box of treasures when you find her; there are a lot of virtues that one can but only credit to her as the Proverbs 31 woman in the Bible.

Growing up with my sister as girls without a father and a brother figure in our lives, we faced a lot of discriminations and challenges in an environment that put preference on a son over a daughter. Our problems were compounded as such that we were brought up by an illiterate widow with no source of income per se.

Our mother having four girls without a boy was a crime and a curse according to the society we come from. We faced rejections, physical abuse, denial of many privileges. Some of our uncles did not believe it necessary for us to go to school. Marriàge at that time was the best option for us according to them. Our problems even multiplied having an uneducated widow mother with not much income to support our education. How best do you think she can raise us up all by herself without any help from family members?

Glory be to God, for His ways are not our ways. I love Psalm 118:5-9: *It is better to trust in God than to trust in human beings for they will disappoint you.* In God's sight both boys and girls are blessings from Him and have equal rights to become whatever they want to become and be great in life. God sent this superwoman at a very young age to stand in the gap and become not just an elder sister but a mother and a father to her siblings. She became our David to stand against the giant Goliath called men and their culture, to defend us, speak for us and our mother. Whatever a man can do my elder sister can do better. Shame to those who believe in devaluing a girl child. She has proved them wrong.

My elder sister's story can't be written in one book. She went through fire, however, as the Bible says in the book of **Isaiah 41:10**:

> **"Fear not, for I'm with you, be not dismayed, for I'm your God. I will strengthen you, yes, I will help, I will uphold you with my righteous right."**

Knowing God was the best thing that happened to us. Lois Hembadoon Adura is a woman whose faith in God is indescribable. She believes that, if God be with you, there is no limit to what you can achieve. She doesn't believe in boundaries or limitations. She believed that, with God she can do all things.

My big sister, I can't underestimate your will-power, therefore I'm not surprised you have written this book. Your boldness, courageous spirit and outspoken ability to voice out your concerns regarding the less privileged cannot be described in words. You are amazing just the way you are. This is just one of your treasures being unveiled again. Keep proving to society that undermining a girl child wrong. Keep soaring high, like the eagle you are. Jesus has got your back. I am super proud of you, iron lady. Your vision and belief for a hope in a female child has pushed you this far. You have fought a good fight and defied all odds in order to bring us, your younger sisters to where we are today. More grease to your elbow. You burnt the candle overnight for us, you are a mother, an aunt, big mummy, a good wife, a super sister par excellence, a friend indeed to many, mentor, minister of God and an umbrella that has shielded all of us with our children...

You are different things to different people at the same time. For us, your family, you are a Messiah. Life would have been miserable without you in our lives. We look up to you, our children look up to their Aunty and big mummy as they call you. Our aged mother is still alive today because of Gods mercy and your sacrifice, care and love. She is blessed to have a daughter like you. We are so blessed to have you in our lives.

As I conclude my tribute, words can't describe your qualities and your relentless efforts in achieving anything your heart so desired. One thing remains unchanged about you, dogged determination, hardworking, keeping a positive attitude in the face of adversaries. Your belief in God puts you above all ordinary women, who don't believe in themselves but depend on what men say about them.

My final word is this: All ye women across the globe arise. Let us show that we are a match to any man. What a man can do a woman can do better. My elder sister is proud to be a girl, as am I. What about you?

Mrs Joyce Ngufan Asuku
(Immediate younger sister).

My big sister, my superhero, my mentor, my mother and my role model.

My superhero, you made life easy for us, your younger ones, from when we were very young. Whilst growing up there was no fear with you around as our defender and guide. I have now come to the full understanding of the proverb that said: *"What a man can do, a woman can do better."* You have proven this beyond a reasonable doubt.

Growing up without a father and an uneducated widowed mother was quite challenging, though she was a very strong woman, and a wonderful mother who never gave up on her girls or remarried and left us to struggle on our own. Only a few people in our family believed in us; the majority used to call us prostitutes and mere girls. My dear big sister, you became an adult at a very young age and took up the role of motherhood challenge, becoming not just a mother but a father to us as well. You are such a passionate, loving, and caring sister and a best friend and confidante to us. Despite the ups and downs of life, you stood by us and we are what we are today because you saw the best in us and brought the best out of us, training all of us through university, an opportunity you didn't get. You never once gave up on us or complained of the burden. You trusted in God and remain a very practical, committed, and active Christian. You put God first.

"Train children in the right way and when old, they will not stray".

Proverb 22:6

You have made a difference not only in our lives but in generations to come. You have proven that gender is no barrier to success. If anyone would ask me about your dogged determination and resilience, I would proudly say, you have put an end to the cultural belief that a girl child is not to be celebrated. Your amazing story should be a wakeup call to all parents and communities across Benue state, Nigeria and Africa.

My big sister's story should be read and celebrated globally, for she broke the chains of cultural curse and poverty in our family. We and our children will never go to bed with an empty stomach again in Jesus name. She sacrificed her happiness, joy, future and career to train us to degree level before she achieved her first degree. What an awesome big sister. If anyone doubts the will-power of a girl child, read about my big sister. Physically she is a woman with a heart of gold, but inside she has a man's spirit.

I am super proud of you my sister Barrister Mrs Lois Hembadoon Adura, formally known as Miss Lois Hembadoon Gbaa. You are my one and only superwoman, my superhero, and role model.

No wonder the Bible says, with God all things are possible.

Doom Stella Atetan.
(2nd younger sister)

My thoughts about my Auntie's life

In this world, there is this proverb that says; *"Opportunity comes but once."* The literal meaning of this proverb is that you should make use of any opportunity that comes your way. Turn any situation you find yourself in round to your advantage, be it negative or positive. Use your perception of the situation and turn it around for your good. *"Overcome evil with good."* **(Romans 12:21).**

Many people miss out on opportunities that present themselves due to their mindset. Whatever doesn't kill you, will make you strong. Fear not, be bold; God has given us the spirit of sound mind, not of timidity or a feeble mind. My Aunty Lois is the perfect example of a woman with a sound mind full of God's wisdom and knowledge. She turned her ordeal into the success story we are reading today.

From what I have heard about her past suffering, alongside what I have observed about her personality, she is a woman that does not hold back once she has set her mind to do something, as is evident in her achievements, and this is a source of great encouragement to me.

As a child, I can only imagine what she went through in life to raise her siblings. My mum (her immediate younger sister) is a benefactor of her sacrifice. Why does society put so much burden on a woman and expect so much from them, when they are given very minimum opportunities in life?

We are all products of a woman's nine-month pains. I have heard many arguments that say without a man as well, you will not be in this world; however, my point is that women are the ones who go through the nine months of pregnancy, and then labour to then raise the child or children, along with all the challenges that this entails.

My Mum, Mrs Joyce Asuku, the second daughter of the Ugber Gbaa family, has told me and my siblings the story of how she and her three sisters suffered in order to become responsible and successful in life. The story that touched my heart the most was that of my mom's elder sister, Aunty Lois Adura. She single-handedly looked after her siblings and sponsored them with little or no support. Despite all the insults thrown at her and her sisters, she did not stop aiming to prove the abusers wrong and show them the potential that God had deposited in her. Thank God, they have all become successful in life.

They are all happily married with good husbands, educated with good homes, and are training their children in the best way possible, so that we, their children, do not go through the problems they faced as children.

My aunty, Mrs Lois Adura is unique, determined, and committed to all of us her family. She is ambitious and no goal is too lofty for her to achieve. She did something remarkable through the grace of God. In 2019, my aunty graduated from the University of Buckingham UK with an LLB, LLM with an award and then proceeded to Nigerian Law school, where she graduated and was called to the Bar as a Barrister and Solicitor of the Supreme Court of Nigeria. All this was done in her fifties - what an awesome achievement to the glory of God. I am super proud of my aunty and "big mummy" as we fondly call her. **She became the first female Barrister in the whole Gbaa family, and the first female in Papa Orkuugh Gbaa's family to achieve a Master of Law degree.**

So, if you are a girl reading this, do not allow the world to underestimate your capability. Be determined to break the limit and achieve your dreams. My aunty has done this and so can you. I have two sisters (Abigail and Favour Asuku) and I am praying to God day and night for them to excel in anything they put their mind to. I want them to turn out like our super strong, role model aunty. Do not let the world tell you that you cannot become something, because that is a big fat lie. My Aunt is the perfect role model to raise a girl's spirit and by reading this book to aim for the top.

Emmanuel Asuku (Nephew).
(Aunty Lois' son, as she fondly calls me)

Tribute for Barrister Mrs Lois Hembadoon Adura

The author, Barrister Mrs. Lois Hembadoon Adura, is my childhood friend, and our relationship is full of God's testimonies in our lives. We lost contact over the years, but God divinely reconnected us. We met again at Universal Reformed Christian Church (URCC) Mabushi Abuja, Federal Capital Territory, Nigeria in the late 1990s, now better and more intimate as born-again sisters, friends, confidantes and this has transformed my life for the better.

There in the Church, she was serving God faithfully. She participated in almost all Church departments from Girls' Brigade, Choir, Sunday School, Girls' Fellowship, usher, etc. Working for God, she touched many lives positively. She gave free accommodation to many. She trained even those not related to her by blood. She took care of the needy, providing for their needs as her means permitted, and she did a lot of charity work, to the extent that she would give even the last money she had on her to someone in need.

She was involved in evangelistic work and gave donations generously to the needy. At times I felt that she was doing too much, as there was a time her box was empty because she donated all her clothes.

Despite all this, many mocked and said many negative things about her, but she kept her faith; she was very focused. There is a saying that when you make God's business your priority, He takes care of your business and little did we know that God was working for her greater tomorrow behind the scenes. An opportunity then came for her to travel outside the country to the United Kingdom (UK). I was so excited because of this breakthrough, but sad because I was going to miss her love and encouragement. At her departure, she gave me virtually all her belongings. When she left, I missed her very much, thinking that this would be the end of our relationship. With many people, when their level changes or rises, they tend to forget their friends or loved ones, but that was not going to be the case in our relationship.

She would always write to tell me what was happening around her. I remember her first salary; she bought items like clothing, shoes, bags, perfumes, etc. and sent to me. Anytime she saw someone coming to Nigeria, she would send something to me.

Oh, what a rare and true friend, one in a million! You are the true meaning of friendship who has added beautiful colours to our friendship and made it very special.

Then, God specially arranged his special son, a very humble, God-fearing, talented, loving and caring, down-to-earth man, Dr. Peter Terfa Adura, as a husband waiting for her, before she arrived in the United Kingdom. The news gladdened my heart and the wedding bells began to ring. The civil wedding was completed, and pictures were sent to me. I was overwhelmed with joy and gladness. I said, indeed, that is how God honours those that seek, trust and serve Him faithfully.

Our friendship became more intimate even though I was still single. She cared much about me and always encouraged me to keep faith that God will do it for me at the appointed time. She did not give up praying and standing in the gap for me. Ultimately God answered her, and she was so happy when I married Dr. Hans Matthias Senwua.

She is part of my success story from the beginning to the end. She kept praying and prophesying that God was going to bless me with a male child for my aged father to see before he left this earth, and it came to pass. God gave me a bouncing baby boy, Daniel Kater Senwua, on the November 6, 2018; indeed, it can only be God and it was like a dream.

Barrister Mrs Lois Hembadoon Adura faced many battles in her life, but as the Bible has stated in Psalm 34:19, many are the afflictions of the righteous, but God delivers him out of them all and she always came out of all of them victoriously. For the battles of the fruit of the womb, God also demonstrated that He is God and His glory no man can share. Glory, honour, and praise to God Almighty, God blessed her with two beautiful, handsome, super-intelligent, well talented, and adorable kids - Miss Doobee Terfa Adura and Prophet Samuel Sefa Terfa Adura.

After our wedding, she and her loving husband invited us to visit them. While we were there, they took very good care of us, accommodated us, fed us with special meals, took us to shops and many places. They gave us lots of gifts and our visit was a memorable one. One month was rather too short for us. We were overwhelmed with their love and hospitality; we appreciate them so much. We have nothing to offer but our prayers are with them. May God Almighty bless and replenish their resources and grant all their hearts desire in Jesus Name, Amen.

Barrister Mrs. Lois Hembadoon Adura is a very hard working and well-determined woman, who will not give up until she achieves her goals. She is never affected by pressure and obstacles, as she believes that they are steppingstones for her success.

She was admitted to the University of Buckingham, United Kingdom to study law. God wanted me to be part of her success story, and I witnessed everything when we visited. She would wake up early in the morning, prepare her kids for school, make breakfast, tidy her house, drop the kids off at school, drive down to Buckingham for her lectures (which is a long-distance), finish, pick up the kids and come back home, prepare meals, take us to places and so it continued. The stress was much, but she kept doing this on a daily basis and was never tired. She never complained and was always happy doing this - what a strong woman she is. I was not surprised when she succeeded with flying colours and immediately did her master's degree in oil and gas law. Then she proceeded to Nigeria to attend law school, where she again passed all her courses with flying colours.

While attending law school, she made time to do additional professional courses in Chartered Mediation and Conciliation and Chartered Secretary and Administration.

These great achievements by this extraordinary woman of God show that delay is not denial; she actually recovered all the years that seemed lost and has taken her career to the highest level. What a mighty God we serve.

All thanks goes to God Almighty and her wonderful and loving husband who stood solidly by her and made sure her dreams came to reality

Dr. Peter Terfa Adura, I respect you a lot. You are so amazing, loving, caring and the strongest pillar for your family. I am so blessed to associate with you. May God Almighty continue to bless and protect you abundantly. May you live long in good health to enjoy the fruit of your labour together. The sky is just the starting point for you, in Jesus name.

Barrister Mrs Lois Hembadoon Adura is very unique, ordained from above, a virtuous woman with a heart of gold, a great achiever, beautiful inside and out, an unshakable prayer warrior, sincere, humble and a prophet of our time. She has had a positive impact on many lives through her generosity.

Many that have visited her home in the UK can testify that she goes out of her way to put smiles on people's faces. She is instrumental in who I am today and is a trusted friend indeed, who refused to quit looking up to her God and ignored all satanic arrows and distractions. I am so privileged and blessed to be part of her success story. She has been a great friend and mentor. Your sacrifices for humanity will be greatly rewarded. You will reap the fruit of your labour. May God continue to bless you beyond your expectations and cause you to see many generations of your children.

Mrs Miriam Member Senwua

A tribute to my mystery woman (An experience I will never forget)

How can I write a tribute to a colossus? How best can I describe this strange and mysterious woman? Strange and mysterious because of her unique way of life which is completely selfless in a selfish world. And how can I make it easy for my thoughts in this tribute to be understood? These are the questions that I struggled to answer while I wrote this tribute.

Like Nishan Panwar said:

"Sometimes, it is not about the journey or the destination... but about the people you meet."

Barr. Mrs. Hembadoon Adura you are not just a friend but a true reflection of what commitment and friendship really is. Being your friend comes with taking an entirely new route that seems difficult yet beneficial to all. You, my friend, have made touching lives positively your ultimate vision. Your amazing determination and dazzling commitment to set goals and the willingness to achieve them, your awesome loving care and ability to give your all to those around you makes you a unique creature. You have shown me by your way of life that "life is not simply that we have lived but more on the difference we made in other people's lives".

You may have forgotten but I cannot forget how in 2006 when I lost everything in fire outbreak, life almost came to a halt. Life was devastating and frustrating. It was not only a difficult situation but the most trying and challenge time in my life. But you became a willing tool that God used to not only dry my tears, but to make me see the future that was waiting. You did something that was not only amazing but cannot be forgotten. You sent me a parcel loaded with everything I needed – clothes, toiletries etc.

Truth is that no material thing can quantify your generous disposition, not only to me but to all those around you.

You are an iron lady, no doubt, but your iron heart is tailored towards making right against the normal shortcuts that is characteristic of today's world. To this end, you are misunderstood.

A tribute to you from me is an endless venture. There's too much to be said, but space won't let me. All I have been trying to do is simply to let you know that I understand, and that I love you. What more can I say to my mystery and strange woman? There's nothing to say! There's nothing to write because there are no words to express exactly how I feel and how grateful I am to you. If wishes were horses, I will give you the world as your footstool because you deserve it. In the absence of that, there's nothing more than to pray and ask God for protection upon your life and family, for answers to your heart desires. This, I pledge on my honour to always do.

I love you my friend and sister.
From my heart, Juliet Wombo.

A diamond class friend

Friends and companions come in different shades and colours. There are those who come to brighten up one's life, whilst others come along to add a tinge of gloom once in a while. The mixture of both types of friends keeps the wheel of life moving and the experiences remain worthwhile. My friend Lois Hembadoon Adura did not come in one colour; she is a rainbow, a constellation of stars exuding internal and external beauty, only adding joy and goodness to all she comes in contact with. She is such a reliable friend that thoughts of her will always make one remember good times which brings tears of joy to the eyes. As I write now, you can imagine a river forming gently in the corners of my eyes.

My friend is one package that comes as a friend and a mother at the same time. When in London, I remember her house being a mini campus, housing different people she cares for. You can walk into her house at any time and be sure to experience that African warmth and hospitality that makes homesickness disappear and makes you feel like a Queen in an alien land. Hers is an open house that welcomes everyone and caters for the needs of all who come by. At times I wonder how she is able to cope with the crowd, but the permanent smile on her face is a perpetual assurance that this is what she loves doing.

I also remember vividly a time when she had to almost empty her account for my sake when I got stuck in paying a particular bill. She will do such things and put an icing on the cake by gently reassuring you that all will be well. She is a generous giver and open-handed confidante. She cares for the needs of all and sundry, follows you up with prayers, and will go to any extent to get you out of trouble. I can go on and on, but I will stop here because I believe no amount of words will ever quantify or fully communicate the goodness reposed in my friend and sister.

All I can say is 'You are a good person and I am sure your reward is on the way.' KEEP BEING GOOD.

Charity Loko.

Tribute from a friend and sister in Christ

I give glory to God for this opportunity and privilege to celebrate the accomplishments of a truly unique and extraordinary individual. I sincerely cherish the opportunity I have been given to write about someone who is not just a friend, but also a sister in Christ, a confidante and my kindred spirit.

Lois Adura has many endearing qualities: her kindness, compassion, and selflessness to name a few. But most of all, many people can attest to her generosity, her liberality in donating gifts to relieve the needs of indigent, ill and helpless people. She's very accommodating and open to everyone who is privileged to meet her. She doesn't discriminate, and she desires to do well to others. She's a woman of consolation, bringing solace to those that are grieving, and hope to children who have lost a parent, providing food and shelter to the homeless and taking time to encourage and counsel those in despair.

She's a voice to the voiceless, unafraid to confront and speak out on behalf of the vulnerable in our society. She has given so much of herself, spiritually, financially, emotionally, and physically. Her liberality in giving, unselfishness, and labour of love will never be in vain.

Her faith in Christ was tested when she was seeking the fruit of the womb; as her knowledge of God increased, the spiritual attacks also intensified. There was nothing the adversaries didn't do to reduce her to nothingness; the constant visits and admission to the hospital, harassment from her employers, attacks from external marital forces to render her weak and exhausted. Each time problems arose; she would rise and face the challenges in prayer. The Bible says the people that know their God shall be strong and do exploits. Her life is built on the Word of God, therefore no weapon formed against her can prosper. What was meant for her harm turned into amazing testimonies and in 2006 after years without the fruit of the womb, she didn't accept the doctor's report that the fibroids were making it impossible for her to conceive. Against all the odds, her adorable baby Doobee was born.

After Doobee's birth, the personal and spiritual attacks were merciless, but this woman of faith was not about to surrender. She had her sights on having a second child. However, test results revealed less than a 5% chance of ever conceiving due to the fibroids and her age. After hearing the consultant's report, she didn't stagger with fear, she clicked her fingers and told him "God forbid". In her asking, seeking, and knocking, first, God showed her the baby boy. Secondly, God asked her why she was praying for something that had already happened. Thirdly, God revealed to Doobee who was seven years old that her mother was pregnant. Each morning they'd pray and thank God for the child until the pregnancy was confirmed in 2013. However, like everything in her life nothing was smooth sailing. The months leading to the birth were very traumatic, and during the last 2 months of the pregnancy I was with her and had first-hand experience of the difficulties she was facing. The pregnancy went to pre-eclampsia, and the doctors told her she had a 40% chance of surviving, while the baby had a 60% chance after the caesarean section.

Prayer was key at this point, even though she was heavily pregnant. We used to pray together and glorify God for His power and love, and we confessed that this problem would be an opportunity to glorify God the more. Baby Sefa was born 6 years after Doobee, although the experience was scary due to her near-death experience. She walked through the valley of the shadow of death, spending three days in a coma and was finally resuscitated and came back to life, to the surprise of the medical personnel who were excited and happy with her recovery.

My friend Lois has been on an extraordinary journey in a life full of trials, tests and self-discovery. She has got here through self-determination and discipline, supernatural abilities, tenacity, and an "I can-do it" mentality. She conquered her fears and despite all obstacles, discouragements and general demands, she dug deep within herself and remained focused. Her positive attitude made her remain optimistic even in times of uncertainty. Any problems she faced she saw it as a miracle in disguise, a springboard to progress and the achievement of her goals.

There's no denying her remarkable accomplishments which can only be described as magnanimous. She has demonstrated that dedication, perseverance, strength of spirit, faith, trust in God and His Word, will bring blessings, victory and success. It's not how you started, it's how you finish that matters, and she finished victoriously. This book is a product of a dogged determination never to give up. I admire her courage.

Finally, marriage is an institution created by God. He said, *"He that finds a wife, finds a good thing and obtains favour from the Lord."* Two can't walk if they don't agree and a house divided against itself cannot stand. Therefore, I would like to say a special thank you to Dr Peter Adura, a wonderful, humble, quietly devoted husband and father. I commend him for standing in the gap during his wife's trying times and the sacrifice he has made for her. His love, support, and encouragement to his wife have yielded fruit in abundance. This virtuous woman is a crown to her husband; he can confidently trust, believe and rely on her. Her adorable children will surely arise and call her blessed.

Barrister Lois Hembadoon Adura, you are moving into a future that's greater than what you are seeing, may God's Word guide your mind. The closer you walk with Him, the higher your level of victories. This has been and will continue to be your story. Once again, congratulations Barrister Lois Hembadoon Adura LLB (Hons) LLM (Master) on your achievement in writing your first book.

Mrs Colleen Marie Hembe
(A friend for 18 years in the UK)

Tribute from a friend

I came into contact with Mrs Lois Hembadoon Adura, then sister Lois Hembadoon Gbaa, in N. K. S. T Church Mabushi Abuja. We were both members of the Church, however sister Lois was so active and dedicated in the service of the Lord in the Church as a youth leader for years, choir member and Girls Brigade coordinator. She was so humble and loving, dedicated and diligent in the things of God and that was what drew me closer to her.

Even then she was so determined to further her education. We both enrolled with the Federal Polytechnic Ugbokolo Abuja branch and started going to part-time school together and when we graduated, she left for the UK for greener pasture. Since then we have kept a close relationship and in constant communication. She values friendship a lot and maintains her friendship at all cost, no matter the distance. When she called to inform me of her intention to go back to school and read law, I was overwhelmed with joy, because I knew of her desire to further her education at any opportunity. We remain in close communication and anytime she is in Nigeria, she calls, and we meet up.

I cannot emphasise enough what a determined woman she is, both in her faith and anything she puts her mind to. When she informed me of her intention to write her first book, I really blessed God for her life. She is such a role model to our generation. There is no dull moment with her; she is full of life, creative ideas, and courage. She doesn't give up until she conquers. Today she can count her blessings and name them one by one. All the many certificates she has achieved are well deserved due to her hard work, dogged determination, and dedication.

I'm very proud of her and encourage all young ladies to emulate her virtues. I am inspired by her faith and determination. Through her, I realised that once you embrace God and you are determined, you can get anything you desire in life, irrespective of your gender or your background. It is not how you start; it is about finishing well. May God continue to uphold you with His victorious hand 'til the end my darling sister.

Rev. Pastor Nelly Gire
(Friend and sister in Christ).

Tribute about my role model, mentor, big sister, inspirer and Big Mummy Lois

There is a saying that says that some human beings are angels in human skin. Barr. Lois Adura actually is an angel in human skin.

Our paths crossed in 2011 through her younger sister Stella Doom Atetan (Nee Gbaa) who happens to be my wife. Our first contact was on the phone and the manner in which we spoke and interacted gave me so much joy and comfort; I knew she was a wonderful person and from that day to date she has not changed.

In 2012 whilst my wife and I were planning to get married she was deeply involved in the project and she made the planning of our marriage look very simple. She was always a step ahead of us and the actualisation of our union came to pass on the 13th of April 2013. She travelled all the way from the UK to witness our wedding ceremony in Nigeria, where she played the role of a host instead of a guest, from the coordination to end of the ceremony.

I envy her energy and passion for her younger siblings and family, but she's actually excited and happy doing all she does for those who come her way, not just to her family members.

As we journey through the marriage institution she has been and still remains the strongest pillar in our household. She has believed in me so much and has shown me genuine love and care. Though she is my sister-in-law, she means much more to me than that.

She's a voice to the voiceless, unafraid to confront and speak out on behalf of the vulnerable in our society. She has given so much of herself, spiritually, financially, emotionally and physically; her liberality in giving, unselfishness and her labours of love will never be in vain.

She has been through the thick and thin and one could say she has seen it all. Through it all she has made it her duty to reach out at all times to put a smile on the face of humanity. I am a living testimony of her gestures. I think her heart beats for humanity. I can't remember her countless deeds to me and my family.

Her faith is very important to her and anyone that knows her will attest to this. She is God fearing, humble, kind and very considerate of others. I could write a book for her deeds to humanity, because facts don't lie.

I wish you well in all your future endeavours and may the light of the Lord shine on you.

Desmond Terlumun Atetan
(Brother-in-law)

My encounter with Mrs Lois Hembadoon Adura

My husband, Dr James Apam, was on a one-year split-site Commonwealth Scholarship for his PhD program in Britain, at Lancaster University, North London, from March 2004 and I went to visit him, on the October 31, 2004. At this time, Mrs Lois Adura & her husband Dr Adura had already got acquainted with my husband through a colleague. As soon as I arrived in Britain, my husband told Madam Lois I was around and asked if we could visit.

Without ever meeting me in her life before, she agreed we should visit her and her family. My husband told her we would visit for a few days then leave for a seminar he needed to attend, but she suggested I should stay behind and wait for my husband. The very next day we arrived at her home, she took me around her kitchen and showed me where all the food items and ingredients were. She said to me, this is your home away from home, feel free. She said, "Madam, in case you want to fix something for yourself, please do since I won't always be in". I stayed behind until after the seminar when my husband came back to meet me and we stayed with them for the Christmas festive period. At that time, Madam Lois was working with Marks & Spencer and studying, however, she still made time to be there for me, my husband, and my husband's colleague who was already staying in their house whilst studying.

I became pregnant with my first daughter Grace Ngohide Apam almost immediately after arriving in Britain. However, being my first pregnancy, I didn't know who to turn to or what to do, especially being far away from home and my mum. I confided in Madam Lois even though she had not been pregnant herself then. She was very supportive both physically and spiritually, praying with me. She informed me about some basic pregnancy-care (sit here, rest, put your legs here, etc).

On Christmas day of 2004, she and her husband took us to Chief Mrs Martha Akiga's (now late) house in London to spend Christmas day. From there, they took us to late Mama Akiga's house for the rest of the celebration of that day. It was in Mama's house she announced to them that I was expecting, and from that day she and her husband would not allow me to touch a pin. They gave me a special seat to relax in at late

Mama Akiga's house to help me keep my feet up. They all gave me special attention, prayed for me and the baby. What a show of love and care all because of Madam Lois.

God used her to buy "Pregnacare Plus" for me and it really helped me, as I was strong all through my pregnancy. She advised me on maternity items that my husband and I should buy, as well as clothes and other essentials for the baby. She gave me gifts of clothes and we felt at home, but it was time for me to return to Nigeria and for my husband to go back to his university, after spending two good weeks with them. She is an exceptionally good, friendly, humble, approachable, God-fearing, and hospitable woman.

At the time we met, she had no child of her own. I remember having a prayer and fasting session program in her house. She is very prayerful and a real go-getter. I believe she prayed and called forth her two lovely kids into existence. I remember her excitedly calling me to tell me she was pregnant with Doobee and she did the same with Sefa as well. She is radical when it comes to her faith and God granted her heart's desires.

When we visited her and family in Southampton in 2013, she said she was doing her first degree in Law and before I knew it, she had graduated and enrolled for a master's program in Law and before I knew it again, she had graduated and was in Nigeria for Law school. Her family and we, her friends, were overwhelmed with joy on her day of call to Bar as a Barrister and Solicitor of the Supreme Court of Nigeria, on the November 27, 2019. It was a tall dream come true for her and in our very presence.

After my first contact with her in December 2004, we have remained connected and great family friends. I have been back to the UK a few times and for each of my trips, we visit her and her lovely family. My husband travels often, so they get to see him more often than me. She has not changed from when we met her from 2004 'til now.

My advice to girls is that nothing good comes easy, so do not give up on any dreams. When God puts a dream in your heart, He will make it come to pass. He gave Joseph dreams of his future. His brothers doubted him, however, when the time came God made it possible. It's never too late.

A practical example of a determined woman is Barr. Mrs Lois Hembadoon Adura. She is a role model for our generation. My counsel to all women is that you should not be discouraged; refuse to give up on your dreams. Whenever thoughts of discouragement come knocking in your heart, look unto Jesus the author and finisher of our faith and encourage yourself in the Lord and reject discouragement. Psalm 118 says it is better to trust in God than trust in human beings that will disappoint you.

Madam Lois is a living testimony of the result of trusting in God wholeheartedly. I believe in Jesus because I have witnessed the miracles in her life. She is a very good advocate for women who need counselling and I have benefitted from her counsel. Talk to her; she is very open, humble, down to earth and approachable.

Bravo to you daughter of Zion. Remain immensely blessed and rapturable! Maranatha!

Mrs Esther Ikwubiela Apam

How I first met
Mrs Lois Hembadoon Adura

I first heard about Mrs Lois Hemhadoon Adura and her husband Dr Peter Terfa Adura, through Rev. Fr. John Ahenakaa Mbanor MSP, a priest colleague of mine with whom I worked in the diocese of Leeds, West Yorkshire, England in 2006, but I actually met her in the Easter week of 2008. I travelled down to their home in Southampton, Hampshire for my Easter break that year. That visit became just the first of many more visits to come, because the Aduras became much more than just acquaintances or friends to me. We became family.

As providence would have it, I was transferred from Huddersfield, West Yorkshire, the diocese of Leeds to Portsmouth diocese in the South, and precisely to Bournemouth, which was not too far from Southampton. It was during this period that I really drew closer and closer to this family. They opened their doors to me and accepted me into their home, and gave me the moral, human, and material support that only one who has had the experience of working away from home, in a foreign country and foreign culture could appreciate.

Dr. Peter and his wife Lois Hembadoon became my brother and sister. They were open to me and me to them. They confided in me and I in them. We shared bits and pieces of our family histories. Their two children, Doobee and Sefa became my niece and nephew respectively and they have known me and addressed me as such ever since.

What can I say about Barrister Mrs Lois Hembadoon Adura from all the years that I have known her? A person's personality is always more complex than appearances. As Martin Luther Junior once said:

"Personality is like a charioteer with two headstrong horses, each wanting to go in different directions."

I acknowledge the fact that it's not always easy to define a person in a few words, especially someone with whom one has interacted over a protracted length of time, indeed over many years, and sometimes even playing the roles of family priest and spiritual director. I have come to know Barrister Mrs Lois Hembadoon Adura as an open-hearted, jovial and welcoming person. She is a good wife, good mother, a good homemaker, and a meticulous home keeper who projects the image of a neat, well-coordinated, and organised person. A visit to her home will prove this to you. She is a good image maker and a woman of the people. She has great organisational ability.

Over the period that I have known her, I have particularly been impacted and challenged by her love for God, her deep prayer life, and her deep spiritual insights, especially in times of personal struggle, both physical and spiritual.

She is blessed with vision. She knows what she wants, sets her goals, and is always determined to achieve these set goals against all odds, whilst always maintaining her strong faith and trust in God to guide and direct her. She has been able to achieve many things in her life, including her many educational qualifications due to God's providence but also through hard work and sheer determination. It is said that two things define one's personality; the way one manages things when one has nothing and the way one behaves when one has everything. I have known this woman in both capacities.

Barrister Mrs L.H. Adura has made a lot of friends in her life including myself. And I can only speak of my experience and what has sustained our friendship for all the time that I have come to know her and her family.

One thing I know about her is that she says things as she sees them. She has no patience for untruthfulness and injustice. She has had a long personal history of struggle against societal, cultural and institutional gender imbalance, rejection, betrayal, and pain - obstacles which her faith and determination have helped her to surmount over the years.

Some people, even her friends, and some family members may disagree with her stance on many issues and I will not be surprised if that becomes a source of conflict. It is part of human nature. But as Albert Camus said:

> **"We continue to shape our personality all our life. If we knew ourselves perfectly, we should die."**

Benjamin Ndayishimiye said,

"If you want to know my personality, look through my bedroom window and see how I act. However, it is always more rewarding to pick what is positive in one's character and leave out the negative."

For in Edmond Mbiaka's opinion

"there is nothing more attractive than a great positive personality. Its beauty never fades away with time."

Rev Fr Vitalis Vaakwagh Kondo, MSP

My encounter and meeting with Auntie Lois

The season beginning with Christmas and leading to the cusp of a new year is one special season. It always brings back the magic of my childhood and animates my dreams, with promises of a new beginning. I look forward to the end of the year as a special time to come away with my family to the manger to adore the Holy

Baby Jesus and rededicate ourselves to Him. Christmas and the new year always remind me of Auntie Lois.

It was in December 2012 that I was blessed to spend quality time with her and her family, although I previously met her briefly whilst in the UK. She has since imprinted herself in my heart as a woman that I look up to and consider as family, and she is my daughter's godmother. That Christmas season in 2012, I was a new bride, thousands of miles from home. She and her lovely family opened their hearts and doors to me and my sweetheart. The conversations, the warmth, the food, the testimonies - there's so much about Auntie Lois that endears her to anyone who gets to know her. I remember attending the New Year's Eve service with her and encountering the Lord Jesus in a way I had never before encountered Him. When you experience transcendence, the friends that walk you through such times take up wings like angels.

She has been amazing; her witness, her heart, her person, her testimony would draw you nigh to seek the one true God. I continue looking up to her as a pillar of faith and an example of a true Christian woman, wife, mother, career-woman, and an emblem of how one woman can positively affect the lives of scores of people across many nations by surrendering herself to the Lord and becoming an instrument in His hand.

Auntie Lois is a woman who uses the boulders strewn in her path to build bridges, launching a pathway to victory not only for herself but for others as well. She is a lady that has not allowed any encumbrance to limit her. The world marvels at the power of a woman who surrenders to God. Things unheard of are accomplished through her by His grace. Ponder upon this, that a virgin conceived and bore Jesus, who is Lord and God! Auntie Lois knows it is Christ in her that is the hope of glory, and her testimony gives us hope and increases our faith. Likewise, our only hope of glory is in Christ Jesus. His Grace is manifest in the life of Aunty Lois, and we celebrate her and give glory to God.

Mrs Karen Erdoo Julius Yina

Tribute to Mrs Lois Hembadoon Adura (nee Gbaa) LLB, LLM, BL, AICMC, ICSAN

I met my wife, Miriam, some time ago in early 2015. Early in our courtship, she told me that she had a friend who now lives in the United Kingdom. That friend was Barr. Mrs. Lois Hembadoon Adura (Nee Gbaa). Miriam and Mrs. Adura had lived in Abuja and interacted at the Universal Reformed Christian Church, Mabushi, Abuja, years earlier.

It was planned that Mrs. Adura would attend our wedding on November 7, 2015, but for logistical reasons, Mrs. Adura could not make it to Nigeria at that time. She was however well represented by her family members and friends in Nigeria.

Soon after Miriam and I got married, Mrs. Adura invited us to stay at her home in the UK. We were there in July 2016. Mrs. Adura and her amiable husband, Dr. Peter Terfa Adura (a UK based first class medical scientist) and their children Doobee and Sefa warmly welcomed us to their Milton Keynes residence. We will never forget the month we spent with the family. We enjoyed unparalleled hospitality and goodwill.

We chose and picked Nigerian and English dishes at will while the visit lasted.

At the time of our visit, Mrs. Adura was in the midst of her studies in Law at the University of Buckingham, UK. Her schedule of activities at that time was an issue of great concern to us. She would wake up at 5:00 am, prepare the children for school, prepare and serve breakfast, take the children to school, dash to Buckingham from Milton Keynes (some kilometres away), rush back to pick the children up from school, prepare and serve lunch and take care of the house in totality. We feared that the barrister-in-training would break down, but that never happened to the glory of God.

Mrs. Adura successfully completed the law degree programme amidst all the pressures around her. She went on to do a Master's in International and Commercial Law, specialising in International Oil and Gas with a Merit and an outstanding performance award. Between completing the first- and second-degree programme and coming to Law School in Nigeria, Mrs. Adura successfully completed her first part of Law school in Bwari Abuja, Nigeria (Bar part 1).

Mrs. Adura puts her family first, so she brought her little son of three years with her to Nigeria and left him with her younger sister in Lagos, as he was too little to be left behind in the UK with the husband. After completing Bar part 1, she applied for a posting to do her Bar part 11 in the Nigerian Law School, Lagos campus. The need to stay near Sefa who was with the Asuku family in Lagos caused her to move to the Lagos campus after one semester in Bwari. This disruption did not prevent Mrs. Adura from completing the law school programme on schedule with flying colours and the consequent call to bar on November 28, 2019 in Abuja. Despite the stringent programme at the law school, Mrs. Adura found time during her weekends to take specialised professional courses culminating in the award of membership of the Chartered Institute of Mediators and Conciliators of Nigeria (AICMC), and Institute of Chartered Secretaries and Administrators of Nigeria (ICSAN). For all these unprecedented achievements we give glory to the Almighty God.

I bear testimony that Barrister Mrs. Adura is a prophetess of the Most High God. During our visit in 2016, she prophesied that my wife, Miriam, in her late forties, would conceive and bear a son. She prayed for us and gave us some baby boy materials even prior to pregnancy, as a point of contact and a sign that it will come to pass. It came to pass as we had a bouncing baby boy on November 6, 2018. The boy, Daniel Kater, is now a bubbling toddler.

On several occasions, Barr. Mrs. Adura called to draw our attention to spiritual issues of which we were yet to be made aware, and these issues came to pass as she saw them and pleaded to God on our behalf. The blessings that have come to us as a result of our relationship with Barr. Mrs. Adura are numerous, and it is not possible to relate all of them in this short space. Our prayer is that the good Lord will continue to bless her and her family and make her a channel of blessing to many as it has always been her lifestyle.

Mrs. Adura's achievements should be an encouragement to womenfolk. Even in today's turbulent and corrupt society, the diligent girl child can still make it in life without cutting corners.

Dr. H. M. Senwua (PhD, MTRCN, JP)

Tribute from a learned colleague at Nigeria Law School, 2019 set

I remember the first day I met Mummy Lois at Law school Lagos campus; my first thought was that why is this woman here? She doesn't even need to be a lawyer; she is already successful. As time went by, I got to observe and know the real Lois Hembadoon Adura. I was so impressed by her determination to pass the Bar finals; she gave it all she had and more. Sometimes I would say, Mummy Lois (as I normally call her), let's take it slow, but she wasn't ready to take a break. She was a source of inspiration to a lot of us at the Nigerian Law School. She assisted many poor students; she could reach out to any students that came to her for assistance. Her generosity was worth mentioning. She was so free with all of us the young ones and everyone at Law school called her mummy. We all had an amazing time with her. I am so glad I came across such a strong, caring and determined woman like you. And I would look forward to reading your book.

Fatima Shehu Binta ESQ.
(Learned colleague).

*****

INJUSTICE AGAINST THE GIRL CHILD:
A Write Up Inspired By This Book

Injustice does not always wear rags. Sometimes it is glamorously vested in the attire of erroneous perception and wrong mentality. Sometimes it is noiseless, unnoticed, inaudible, yet it ravages swiftly and deeply.

Whistle editing Sister Lois' book, I have identified an injustice; to be quiet would be to support its perpetuation. This is injustice against the girl-child.

When she dreams big, she is told, "Remember that you are just a girl," as if dreams are gender sensitive. When she achieves her big dream, she is asked incredulously, "But how were you able to do it?" Some conclude that her success must have been bought at the expense of her innocence and integrity, as if she is not con-figured for or capable of noble achievements.

When she is trying to decide on her future, taking her time and discerning carefully to avoid mistakes, there is pressure from all directions.

"What are you waiting for? When are you settling down? Look at 'so, so and so' your friend, she is with her second child and my friend 'so, and so' are now Grandmothers."

After some years of marriage, if her period is punctual and committed to its monthly visit, people start asking her what's wrong, because in the misguided thoughts of the ignorant, when there is a delay in conception, clearly it can only be the fault of the woman.

"Yes, it is her fault, because our son is as solid as a rock and he can't possibly be at fault. His virility is unquestionable!"

Some in-laws even begin to put God to the test by mocking, scorning, blaming and threatening her. If eventually, she gives birth and it is a girl, then some will start the chorus of loons and the refrain of exotic misfits, "Make sure your next child is a boy," as if she determines gender and controls nature.

If she has only female children, then another round of scoffing ensues, "We need a boy from you. We need someone to continue the family name."

What if she has boys and girls and they are exhibiting questionable conduct? The blame again is on her - she has not trained them well. And if they are well behaved? Well, obviously the credit goes in the other direction.

For those who think in this deluded manner, let us pray to the Lord: Lord in your mercy, grant them some sense.

If she is a woman with creative ideas, affirmed and determined, then she is alleged as controlling her husband. She is classed as domineering. If she is simple, unassertive and always affirming, she is termed as clueless and non-supportive.

If her marriage does not work out, it is her fault; she is to be blamed. Obviously, every broken relationship is a woman's fault, because she was not able to endure, she was not able to build her home. Then she is compelled to bear the stigma of a failed marriage, but if she wants to try another relationship, she is classed as second hand and therefore her value must drop. However, it is not a big deal for a man in the same situation. After all, he is a man, and a man is a man by definition.

Lord, save us from a way of thinking that does not make sense, is hostile to truth and incompatible with justice.

What a pity!

I could go on and on, such is my strength of feeling, but I choose to leave the rest to your own conscience. Friends, when we preach justice, we must seek it in every gamut of life not just in selective areas.

(I felt inspired to share these thoughts when I read the story of Barr. Lois Adura, who together with her mother and siblings had to cope with so much rejection and difficulty, simply for being who they are - girls in a society that would prefer them to be boys, whether useful or otherwise).

I, Fr. Emmanuel Okami, say "NO!" to gender injustice. I respect, honour and celebrate a girl-child as much as a male-child.

Fr. Emmanuel Okami
WOLM, Milton Keynes, UK

8

CONCLUSION

"We might be thrown into the blazing furnace. But the God we serve is able to bring us out of it alive."

Daniel 3:17

God will work out His plans for your life as a woman. You don't have to work it out. You don't have to make it happen in your own strength or fight all the battles. Believe God's word in your situations. Let God work out His perfect plans for your life. He can do it better than you can. He knows the best design and pattern He has for your life. Believe and receive His blessings that add no sorrow to it. Better is the end of a thing than the beginning. It doesn't matter how poorly we all started; it is the greater success we achieved that matters most. Women are created for a purpose and we must fulfil our purpose in life through God's amazing grace.

Each day we have many decisions to make. Choosing to do the right thing each time can be challenging. The right things aren't always easy things. We might have to overcome the emotions we feel. We might have to go against what we really want to do. But doing the right thing, the things that God wants us to do, is vital if we're going to follow Him.

In the Bible, Joseph was a man who chose to do the right thing at many points in his life. When Potiphar's wife tried to seduce him, he said no because he knew it was wrong. When his brothers turned up begging for help, he chose to show mercy. This might have been a really hard choice for Joseph to make. His brothers plotted to kill him, had thrown him down a pit, and then sold him into slavery while pretending to their father Jacob that he was dead. Joseph could have chosen to live a life of resentment. He could have held a grudge against his brothers and refused to help them. But he chose to do what was right in God's eyes. Firstly, he forgave them. Joseph said:

> "And now do not be distressed, or angry with yourselves, because you sold me here; for God sent me before you to preserve lives."
>
> **Genesis 45:5**

Secondly, he chose to provide for them. He said:

> "You shall settle in the land of Goshen, and you shall be near me, you and your children and your children's children, as well as your flocks, your herds, and all that you have. I will provide for you there since there are five more years of famine to come so that you and your household, and all that you have, will not come to poverty."
>
> **Genesis 45:10-11**

It's important that we do what's right in God's eyes. He'll give us the wisdom and strength we need to be able to do it.

My final counsel and notes to the girl child and women who had and are suffering from the paradox of unfavourable culture

Dear beautiful, unique and amazing girls,

Listen, though every human being craves to be loved and accepted just the way they are, the world will never give you that unconditional love and acceptance because it simply doesn't have it. To the world, you are always a mark short of becoming 'one of them.' You're just a girl: not good enough, not smart enough, not rich enough. It's always this or that. You try so hard and work to negate their view of you, to become one of them. No matter how hard you try, you can't seem to gain approval and win their love.

STOP! You're not called to be a male; appreciate who you are and live your dream.

You are set apart:

> "But you are a chosen race, a royal priesthood, a holy nation, God's own people, in order that you may proclaim

the mighty acts of him who called you out of darkness into his marvellous light."

1 Peter 2:9

The Lord loves you with an everlasting love, regardless of your sex. He takes delight in you.

"For the LORD takes pleasure in his people; he adorns the humble with victory."

Psalms 149:4

You need to constantly remind yourself that nothing can ever separate you from His love.

"nor height, nor depth, nor anything else in all creation, will be able to separate us from the love of God in Christ Jesus our Lord."

Romans 8: 39

When you accept the love that the Father has lavished on you, you will appreciate who you are. When you know you are loved and cherished so much that Christ had to die for love of you, you can accept His love and surrender to Him and be crucified to the world."

"May I never boast of anything except the cross of our Lord Jesus Christ, by which[a] the world has been crucified to me, and I to the world."

Galatians 6:14

In this world there's so much injustice and inequity, so much that is unfair. We should continue praying for His Kingdom to come and to shine His light. The other day, I had a conversation with the Lord about something that I felt was an injustice I was suffering from. It went along the lines of, 'Lord I know you don't like this happening to me... your beloved daughter and I don't like it (in fact I detest it). Since we both agree we do not like it, how do you expect me (mere mortal) to cope?'

He whispered gently and said to me:

"My grace is sufficient for you, for power is made perfect in weakness. So, I will boast all the more gladly of my weaknesses, so that the power of Christ may dwell in me."

2 Corinthians 12:9

I was led to contemplate our Lord's passion. Christ lives in us and has given us His Holy Spirit. When we suffer, He does not leave us on our own. He suffers alongside us and invites us to offer our sufferings up to Him. He gives us beauty for ashes, strength for fear, gladness for mourning, and peace for despair.

> "The spirit of the Lord GOD is upon me because the LORD has anointed me; he has sent me to bring good news to the oppressed, to bind up the broken-hearted, to proclaim liberty to the captives, and release to the prisoners; to proclaim the year of the Lord's favour, and the day of vengeance of our God; to comfort all who mourn; to provide for those who mourn in Zion to give them a garland instead of ashes, the oil of gladness instead of mourning, the mantle of praise instead of a faint spirit. They will be called oaks of righteousness, the planting of the LORD, to display his glory."
>
> **Isaiah 61:1-3**

He alone can turn even our sufferings around and make them work for our good.

> "We know that all things work together for good for those who love God, who are called according to his purpose."
> **Romans 8:28**

He can bring purpose from our pain and lead a mission from our mess. Against this backdrop, when you experience suffering and trials, it is not about you. It is about what God wants to do with you and through you; He wants to be glorified in you. In all your experiences, your hurts and joys, Christ is leading you.

The question is where to?

When God called Abraham to leave his fatherland, he did not give him a map, but a word and a promise. Obedience is the key that unlocks the reward. Even for the righteous, this reward does not come immediately. Abraham waited 25 years for Isaac. Waiting can suck, it is no fun and can be boring. If Father Abraham had cultivated the attitude that waiting is boring and suspended purposeful living, then he would not be our Father in faith. Instead, he lived his best life every day, even between the promise and its fulfilment. And so, you need patience in your walk with the Lord to receive the promise in the fullness of time. As children of Abraham, we too can believe and obey as we wait on Him day by day. Despite the pain and the strain, the glory is sure if you believe and endure to the end. You too can live your best life now despite the pain that you have been through. Sometimes, it is because of that pain that something glorious rises from the ashes to glorify God.

Do not hold back, live your life knowing who you are in Christ, relish it, and let His light shine.

****

Recommendations and possible solutions to end male child syndrome

I suggest some intervention programmes to help eradicate this evil side of the culture and focus on the positive aspect of it. In the quest to check the consequences of son preference in our community (TIV) therefore, I make an appeal to our Royal father (Begha u Tiv, Orchivigh Prof James Ayatse) to consult the traditional chiefs and arrange for a training program for them on intervening by creating an awareness in their communities to help educate parents about the importance of a female child as well as a male child, alongside programs that will foster education for the girl child and also consider the plight of widows and their daughters.

It is high time the Tiv traditional council looked into this culture and redressed it. We, the daughters of Tor Tiv, through this book seek to plead with our Royal father (Begha u Tiv, Orchivigh Prof James Ayatse) to consider looking into this long-standing culture and redressing it because the prevalence of male child preference within the Tiv community has a huge impact on female children. When you speak to a victim of this phenomenon, you can't hold back tears. We cannot replace male children, but we deserve love, kindness, and dignity as well.

Recently our Royal father has dedicated Tiv land back to God. Therefore, some of these unnecessary pressures on female children should be eased. We your daughters, therefore, are pleading with you and your council of traditional chiefs, to consider reviewing this cultural structure of patriarchy, to consider a family where a father has gone to be with the

Lord without a male child, and to not deprive his daughters and his widow of their rightful inheritance, and to create an awareness to help men stop maltreating their wives for their inability to bear a male child to carry the family name.

The desire for a male child has resulted in situations where husbands keep pressuring their wives to have more children, which in turn predisposes the health of the wives to danger. At times when these measures fail to produce the desired results, some of these men resort to polygamy in the hope that the other women would give them sons. They jeopardise the family peace in search of that elusive boy.

****

An appeal to our Royal father: Your Royal Highness,

We are pleading for a stop to the harassment of women without male children in Tivland; enough is enough. We are crying out for help from our Paramount Ruler to address this issue of male child syndrome among the Tiv community. Women cannot carry on suffering for their inability to bear a male like this through no fault of their own.

Another approach to help tackle this issue could be to view not just adulthood but childhood through the prism of gender. This means subjecting all planning, programming, and evaluation of development activities geared to children to gender analysis and fostering vigorous compensatory programmes to remedy the effect of early male-biased approaches. Most importantly however, it means acknowledging the girl's basic human right to a gender-just childhood and identifying and condemning those factors that discriminate against girls in the rearing process.

Also, the Benue state government can encourage Non-Governmental Organisations (NGOs) to join in the consciousness-raising for the whole society on the value of girls and women, the need for equal education, and health care for boys and girls, and the need for legal changes to promote male-female equality. Though the culture may not be easily changed, over time culture does systematically adapt to new changes. In fact, there should be the establishment of state, local government, and ward council working groups of every family head in Tivland, formulated to promote action strategies to reduce harsh treatment to widows and their daughters by family members when their husbands pass away. They should also appeal to husbands to be more considerate to their wives for the inability to bear a male child or children at all. No woman wants to be barren or have only one sex of child.

The ministry for education should introduce and encourage gender-sensitive curricula in schools and strengthen the ethics both in schools and Churches to avoid gender discrimination and bring it to the barest minimum if possible.

*****

My honest prayers for all female children, women with only daughters, widows, and barren women in Tiv land using myself as a point of contact.

My prayer for all female children who have been rejected, barren women who have been forsaken, widows who have been maltreated and deprived of their inheritance, women who suffer injustice because of their inability to bear a male child and all women who are suffering presently under the curse of patriarchal tradition:

❖ The Lord will build walls of protection around you in Jesus' name. As the mountains surround Jerusalem, so will the Lord surround you and shield you and your loved ones from any form of danger and wicked family members who use unfair culture to the detriment of vulnerable women in Jesus' name.

❖ As the Lord restored the fortunes of Zion, and with His Risen Life, so will your fortunes be restored, and your mouth will be filled with laughter and your tongues with songs of joy in Jesus' name. My fortune has been restored; yours too is guaranteed in Jesus' name.

❖ I pray that the Rock of Ages will continue to protect you, with your loved ones, and deliver you from the nets of the fowlers in Jesus' name. Your protection is guaranteed in Jesus' Mighty Name.

❖ Though the giant called "a male-dominated culture" may be in our way to hinder, God will surely give us victory in Jesus' name.

❖ The God of Zelophehad's Daughters is forever your God and you will succeed in Jesus' name above all odds. (Numbers 27:1-11).

❖ God will remember you as He remembered the Widow of Zarephath. (1 Kings 17: 8-24).

❖ No one shall miscarry or be barren in your land, I will fulfil the number of your days. (Exodus 23:26).

❖ The Lord will make you the head not the tail in Jesus' name. (Deuteronomy 28:13).

❖ You will not labour in vain, nor your children. (Isaiah 65:23)

❖ No one will pluck you out of my hand, says the Lord of hosts. (John 10:29).

❖ I will restore to you the years that the swarming locust has eaten. (Joel 2:25).

❖ Fear thou not, for I am with thee. (Isaiah 41:10).

❖ I have loved you with an everlasting love. (Jeremiah 31:3).

❖ For I know the plans I have for you says the Lord. (Jeremiah 29:11).

❖ A song of our victory. Sing this song (I have paraphrased it):

> "Once I was a victim (sinner) but now I am no more, singing hallelujah to my Lord ... Oh, hallelujah singing, halle-lujah singing (x2), Hallelujah to my Lord."

EPILOGUE

I am very excited and super proud of being a woman regardless of the cultural stigma. How about you my amazing sisters? Praise the Lord. God has not made a mistake by creating women. We are unique and precious in His eyes. See yourselves as such. **Jeremiah 29:11.**

You have all read the beautiful stories in this book, enjoyed them, at some point you became a bit emotional about some of the stories, but what's better than all of those stories are the ones you are continuing to write with your life daily after reading this book.

If you are like me, I'd ask myself after reading this book called *"Saved by Grace"* – *So what do I do next?* Do I have the determination, courage when faced with adversity, fighting spirit and a firm faith in God? If these are the tough questions going through your mind right now, honestly the answer can be an easy one.

Let me tell you what I do when I don't know what to do to push forward with my dreams. I trust God being in control and by faith usually just try to figure out what the next step is and then do that. I know it sounds too simple, too formulaic; it seems like there must be more to it, however, there isn't. This is different with individual people; my strategy, my faith and belief may not work for you, but you will acknowledge things in your life that have God's fingerprints on them. You will know which ones do and which ones don't. Seek God's approval in all these. Pray fervently, trust and obey His leading. Seek for counsel from those more experienced than you.

Even though everyone is different, choose the one thing that already lights you up when you do it; something that makes you happy when you do it, something that you feel like you were made to do and then do lots of that. We are unique in our own ways; don't try to do what your friend is doing; that might not be your calling and your talent might not be in that.

A couple of stories you have read in this book differ in their circumstances, and their approach in solving their problems was different from the others. Focus on your strength and ask God for directives. We are all different and so is our individual problem. But together we can achieve anything by sharing our testimonies and being our sisters' keepers. Stop tearing each other down; let's love one another and build ourselves through the Word of God and moral support. Let's appreciate ourselves, life is too short to waste on envying another and being jealous of a sister.

Our God is good all the time and all the time our God is good. Glory.
Mrs Lois Hembadoon Adura Esq

Printed in Great Britain
by Amazon

45323013R00163